ONLINE PREDATORS

A PARENT'S GUIDE FOR THE VIRTUAL PLAYGROUND

DEPUTY CHIEF MIKE SULLIVAN

ONLINE PREDATORS
by DEPUTY CHIEF MIKE SULLIVAN

Printed in the United States of America

ISBN 978-1-60647-741-0

www.xulonpress.com

ONLINE PREDATORS
A Parent's Guide for the Virtual Playground

The opinions in this book are mine and are not to be attributed to any other person or agency. They are not meant as the opinions of any local, state, or federal law enforcement agency. Although I work in the law enforcement field any opinions in this book are not meant to be reflected as official opinions from any of the agencies I have been employed by or work in cooperation with during my regular enforcement activities.

DEDICATION

This book is dedicated to the men and women who are members of the Internet Crimes Against Children Task Force. Each day they work to protect our children from online predators. Their work environment is both physically and emotionally dangerous each and every day. It is also dedicated to Ernie, Michelle, Jen, Christine, Lindsey, Cristina, Pete, John and the rest of the men and women of the National Center for Missing and Exploited Children. Their whole purpose in life is to protect the world's children.

A special thanks to Dawn, my editor, without her assistance this book would not be a reality.

ONLINE PREDATORS
A Parent's Guide for the Virtual Playground

CONTENTS

CHAPTER 4: SOCIAL NETWORKING SITES

CHAPTER 5: WHERE CAN I TURN FOR HELP?

CONCLUSION

CHAT GLOSSARY

FOREWORD

By Teri Schroeder
CEO/Founder, i-SAFE America

Predatory acts against our children are among the most heinous of crimes perpetrated within our society. Historically, communities have collectively taken deliberate and specific actions to protect their children from these terrible acts. These protective actions include education, such as teaching children to be wary of strangers, to recognize and avoid dangerous situations and to cry for help when they feel threatened.

Our nation is now faced with technological advancements that allow even the youngest of children to have access to the internet. Students today explore the wonders of the world by transporting themselves through cyberspace. They can travel to the brightest, most intellectual domains of the universe, and conversely, they may travel to the darkest, most detestable realms of the human imagination; and they travel this world alone. A universal paradigm shift has occurred in the methods and means available to child predators in pursuit of their prey. Thus, a universal paradigm shift has occurred on the preventative tactics that we employ in our efforts to protect our nation's youth against these predators.

Our children now live in two diverse worlds: their physical world and the world of cyberspace. As such, they essentially live in two cultures that often conflict. Many of the lessons learned in the physical world don't seem relevant in cyberspace as these children reach out to strangers as friends. It is essential that children, as they travel their world of cyberspace alone, be provided with the knowledge and tools they need to independently recognize and avoid dangerous situations online; to actively engage learned proactive techniques to more safely interact with strangers online; to critically appraise situations in which they find themselves; and to react appropriately when they find themselves in uncomfortable, compromising or threatening situations.

It is widely recognized and accepted that the main activity of young cyber citizens is online two-way communication. That communication consists of chat, email, blogging and instant messaging. The internet affords the opportunity for two-way communications, but the computer does not know whether the users communicating are children or adults. This means of communication allows users, regardless of age, gender or socioeconomic status, to openly and freely exchange ideas and information. Our nation's youth have now coined a new term for "hanging out with my friends" (the new term is "chillaxin'" which combines "chillin'" with "relaxin'") and actively searching for new friends is done through a click of a mouse.

Historically, when parents taught their children to recognize and avoid dangerous situations, those situations were based on tangible, physical elements within their community. Now, danger lies in an amorphous cyber-world cloaked in the illusion of anonymity.

The internet has broadened a child's ability to meet other people and acquire "friends." Historically, children made friends at school, through family acquaintances and from participating in community organizations. A child is no longer confined to the local community in order to socialize and gain friends; literally, cyberspace eliminates all geographical barriers and frees a child to roam the world in search of that one, special "friend." Predators are also free to roam.

The degree of difficulty for parents to monitor, or to simply meet, their child's friends has increased tremendously. Parents routinely lock their doors at home each night to keep intruders out; schools monitor persons who enter the campus. There are innumerable, vulnerable children who are isolated, lonely and bored who constantly search the internet for other children with whom they can make friends and chat. As these children search the web for friends, so too the predator searches the web for prey. The predator will find the child, the child will find a "friend," and the outcome will be devastating.

I applaud Mike Sullivan for his dedicated service and leadership in educating and empowering parents concerning the online dangers and the importance of "cyber parenting" in today's global environment. This is a book that every parent must have on their bookshelf. Share this book with a neighbor or loved one. The return on the investment could be the life of your child or someone you know.

***i-SAFE America** (http://www.isafe.org) is a nationwide nonprofit foundation focusing on internet safety for students. Founded in 1998, the group launched its Safe Schools Education Initiative and Outreach Campaign in 2002.*

INTRODUCTION

In most of the homes around the world the true computer experts are our children. They spend hours on the computer each day and are not intimidated by the latest technology. They can navigate the computer, the internet, chat rooms, instant messages, blogs, text messages, camera-enabled cell phones, and web cameras as if it were second nature to them. While most adults feel challenged by the numerous icons, menu choices and social networking sites, our children feel empowered by these elements of the cyber world. Children are drawn to the ability that online activities can provide to announce their presence to the world. The vast majority of online sessions are pleasant experiences with positive results for homework assignments, term papers, research projects and instant messages confirming what is the most popular movie currently showing or who is their date for the prom. Unfortunately, some of the sessions are not as innocent and can have devastating effects on our children. Sexual predators have found the computer and the internet to be the perfect place to locate their next victim, trade contraband images and movies of the molestation of children and elicit support from other sexual predators.

I have been in law enforcement for almost 30 years. During my career, I have worked as a detective in a cyber crimes unit and as a supervisor of investigators engaged in the identification of sexual predators using the internet to locate victims. One of my duties is to create training classes and curriculum for police officers so that they may learn how to locate, identify and prosecute sexual predators who use the computer and the internet to victimize children. Probably the most valuable training I have received is that of a parent of two children growing up with computers and the internet. Just like many of today's parents, I have worried about where my children venture online. What is my child doing online? What is my child seeing online? Who is my child contacting online, and the most important question, *is my child safe online*? These are the concerns that led me to work in the high tech crimes area, write the Safe Kids Program for children in the fourth to sixth grades, testify before the Child Online Protection Act committee and participate in Internet Safety Nights for parents at schools and community centers. This book is an outgrowth of the questions and concerns raised by the parents during those internet safety presentations.

The main questions have not changed since I started in computer crimes over 15 years ago. However, new questions and websites have entered the mix. Questions about safe websites, safe chat sites and age appropriate locations on the web are now mixed with questions about the use of social networking sites or concerns about text messages being exchanged during school exams. Parents want to know what information is safe to include when their children fill out an online profile. What I hope to accomplish with the information in this book is to give the average parent a fighting chance to monitor their child's online activities and make them as safe as possible. The question I probably hear most often from parents is, "Can I buy a piece of software and install it on my computer and know that I have done everything I can to protect my child?" Unfortunately, the answer to that question is, "No!" As parents, we protect our children with helmets, elbow- and kneepads when they want to learn how to ride a bicycle or roller blade. Likewise, we supply our children with the necessary clothing to protect them from the cold or rain. However, there is no "silver bullet," no one piece of software that will protect your child from all online dangers. There are pieces of software that can be combined with good old-fashioned responsible parenting skills to give any parent some peace of mind that they have done everything they can to make it safer for their child to be online. One active parent can be a most effective deterrent to online predators.

The predator relies on keeping their contact with your child a secret. We will look at this online "grooming" in more detail later in the book, but keep in mind that your strongest weapon against an online predator is teaching your child to trust you and communicate with you. The last thing an online predator wants to hear from your child is, "I have to check with my parents." That statement alone can drive many of the online predators away from your child. Unfortunately there are all too many unprotected or ill-equipped children on the internet. Online predators prefer to terminate contact with children willing to discuss online actions with their parents. Instead, they will seek one of the millions of children looking to share in an online relationship with a "secret friend."

*The strongest weapon an online predator has against your child is **secrecy**. The strongest weapon a parent has against online predators is **communication**.*

CHAPTER 1: THE BASICS

I. Learning a New Language

Many parents today feel the computer and the internet are their enemies. It is a foreign land with strange rules, an unintelligible language and a personal agenda meant to frustrate anyone over the age of 16. Take comfort in the fact that you are not alone. Not everyone can navigate a computer operating system and the internet like a junior high student. Also, keep in mind that often their friends have gone out before them and found the music file, image or movie they are looking for and given them directions on how to find and download the file. As parents we do not have that type of technical support network. The terms and phrases our children use sometimes seem incoherent to us. They talk about texting, trading files, MP3s and flash drives.

Throughout this book I will try to keep the terminology simple and not use too much technical jargon (also known as "geek speak"). As often as possible I will use plain and simple English to describe tasks, programs or hardware items contained within your computer. If a “geek term” is necessary I will try to include a plain English version of the item or its intended purpose. At times I hear parents saying that using the computer and the internet is as difficult as learning a new language. That is truer than they know. Many of us do not readily understand terms such as RAM, gigabyte, terabyte, peer to peer or IMing. Even though we may not understand the terms or how the processes work, we probably have made use of some of them. You surely have used the RAM in your computer while surfing the internet or been glad for the gigabytes of storage space on your hard drive as your children fill them with music and movie files. Take comfort in knowing you are not the only parent yelling at your children to stop chatting or texting and come to dinner.

II. Component Terminology

Let’s start with a few simple terms that you may hear when you’re attempting to purchase a new computer or your child is asking to upgrade your current computer for their school work. Upgrade is usually “child speak” for, “I have run out of storage space for music and movies and you need to buy me a bigger hard drive so I can store more files." Probably the most common reason for upgrading is related to storage. Children, plus music and movie files, equals a need for massive amounts of storage space.

When you are looking for a new computer the main terms you will hear are processor speed, amounts of RAM and hard drive size. There are many other features to consider, but for now let's focus on these three.

Processor speed can be misleading as each company computes the speed differently and they vary by chip manufacturer. The fact is, almost any currently offered computer will get you online. For the purposes of this book and keeping things simple, I am not going to break down the function of every component. Instead, I am going for a general understanding of how they interact to help make your computer use pleasant and efficient.

When your child wants to surf the web and listen to music and you want them to do their homework, the processor speed comes into play. The processor speed combined with the amount of RAM will determine how fast your computer truly works. Currently the industry is changing from single core processors to dual core. If you are looking for a new computer you may want to look for one that is a dual core model with enough specifications to be Vista compatible. These two items will help extend the useful lifespan of your computer. Currently the operating systems on most PCs are changing from Windows XP to Windows Vista. Making sure you purchase a Vista compatible computer means you will be able to update the operating system from XP to Vista or you may order it directly from the manufacturer with Vista already installed. While it is important to consider lifespan and compatibility issues when choosing an operating system, it is best to select a computer with the most popular current operating system you are comfortable using right now. Sometimes that may mean getting one that has been around for a while and not the most current version. New operating systems need time to sort out the bugs and glitches. It might be better to let someone else deal with the frustrations of the new operating system, report the problems and allow the fixes to take place. This way when you do get around to buying or upgrading to the newer operating system it will be significantly more stable.

The screen captures shown in this book are from Windows XP. However, I have taken my own advice in regard to when to buy a new operating system. I have purchased several new computers with the Vista operating system and given them to some of my colleagues at work. I am learning from them what the ups and downs of Vista are before I commit to buying a computer with Vista installed.

Macintosh users disregard the above information concerning the operating system. I will not get into the debate over which format is better, PC or Mac. I have used both and know each works best in certain areas. However, for the needs of most families either format will work. Just know that not all software companies that write protective software for children make it available in both formats. In regard to the processor speed, any speed over 1.8 GHz will work fine for getting on and off the internet.

The true test of the processor speed occurs when your child is launching multiple applications at the same time. The more applications opened, the harder the processor needs to work. First, you always have the operating system running. Second, you should have an antivirus program to protect your computer from viruses and Trojans. Then your child launches a browser (Internet Explorer or Mozilla Firefox are two of the more popular ones) to visit the internet in order to gather the research for their homework assignment. Some form of word processing program (Microsoft Word or WordPerfect are pretty common) will also need to be running to write the paper. Of course, they will need to view graphics and listen to music while doing their homework. The media player and viewing of graphics will add to the strain on the processor.

The RAM installed in your computer assists the processor in its mission. The more RAM, the more assistance it can lend to the processor. How much RAM is needed? Currently I would suggest two gigabytes of RAM as a minimum. This will give you enough to run the latest operating systems, browse the internet and view websites. It should also cover you for the increases in demand over the lifespan of the computer. If you want, you can up the amount of RAM to four gigabytes. This will not only allow for the above operations but will also assist with the display of graphics or videos on websites. Most graphic cards will come with some RAM built into the card, but increasing the size of the RAM in your computer can only help. However, like taking medicine, there is a limit to how much RAM is good for you and a point at which it becomes excessive. Check with the specifications of the computer you own or are buying and ask about the upper limit that actually will work on your computer or with your operating system. There are limits and buying RAM above those limits is just a waste of money.

Now for the one part that always keeps us chasing new technology: the size of the hard drive. I know this is a bad joke, but size really does matter when it comes to hard drive space. It is true that hard drive space is one of the more difficult factors to deal with when it comes to buying a computer.

III. Selecting a Computer

Recently my nephew was heading off to college and he needed a computer for school. My sister and he decided to purchase a laptop and contacted me for assistance. I walked my sister through most of the flyers from computer outlets and national retailers, and we also looked on companies' websites. After explaining processor speed, dual core and dual core2 models, amounts of RAM and wireless networking/Ethernet card (I will come back and explain these two in a moment), we arrived at hard drive size. I advised them that a 100 or 120 gigabyte hard drive was probably more than large enough for any school assignments, term papers or speeches. Most of these are text documents and take up very little space.

However, my nephew wanted to be sure it would hold all the music from his CD collection. We settled on a 160 gigabyte hard drive and a model that contained a CD/DVD writer (also called a burner). The CD/DVD burner will allow my nephew to store his school material on CD or DVDs and will leave most of the space on the hard drive for his music. All I can say here is pick your battles; at least he is in school and studying. You can try, but the fact is when they start to use the computer they will start adding music and movies and fill up the hard drive. I remember when a 500 megabyte hard drive was huge and I never thought I would fill it. As file sizes have grown from several kilobytes to 5 megabytes for a song and half to three quarters of a gigabyte for a movie, you can see how quickly a 160 gigabyte hard drive can be filled. This year will see the size of hard drives on home desktop models move into the one terabyte range. Currently CDs hold 650 megabytes at the cost of about a dime each when purchased in bulk. This makes burning the data to CDs a cheap format for backing up large amounts of school work and freeing up room on the hard drive.

DVDs are a little more expensive but are necessary for files over 650 megabytes.

IV. Understanding Wireless

Earlier I mentioned that we added a wireless networking/Ethernet card to the laptop. At home most families will connect the computer to a modem and access the internet via a built-in Ethernet card. Basically, this is a card that is built into the computer, with a slot for the RJ45 cable to plug into and connect the computer to your modem. The card will have the necessary software installed to recognize the connection to the modem and allow you access to the internet.

However, with my nephew going off to college he needed the wireless card to access the wireless network on campus. Instead of plugging the computer into a modem via a cable, the wireless card allows the computer to connect wirelessly to the school's network and then onto the internet. Wireless technology allows the computer to be mobile and connect via any open wireless network. There are two different types of wireless networks. There is Wi-Fi which can be free and there are wireless cards that work with cellular telephone technology. The latter usually requires the purchase of an "aircard" and a monthly fee to allow a connection. Companies such as Starbucks, Caribou Coffee, Panera Bread Company and some locations of McDonald's supply a free wireless network for use by its customers during their time at the restaurants. Personally, I have found that working from these locations, away from distractions like the constant ringing of phones at the office, is a great way to get work done. They also allow for a free method of staying in touch with the office via email. The downside can be an overly gracious supply of caffeinated soda and delicious oatmeal raisin cookies. This makes these sites good for work, bad for the waistline. **Personal Rule:** one visit, one cookie (and, no, my wife did not have anything to do with making that rule). But that does bring me to a point about additional information later in this book. When you see the phrase **"Personal Favorite"** it will indicate that I personally have used the software I am describing on my own computers and like the way it works enough to recommend it as my own **Personal**

Favorite. I will explain the features I like and why I use the software. It does not mean it is the only software on the market or necessarily the best piece of software just because I use it. What it does mean is that I feel confident recommending this software because I have used it and seen how it works to make my own computers and children safer. Also note that I purchased all of the software I discuss in this book just like any other user and I did not receive any free software or payment to select the software or to recommend it.

Originally, like most law enforcement officers, I looked at these wireless networks as a bad thing, envisioning predators flocking to the free wireless networks. However, that is not what is happening in real life. This is only a personal observation, but I believe the types of crime that sexual predators are committing demand a level of privacy that does not exist at these locations. The sexual predators cannot sit and look at pornography, and certainly not child pornography, without fear of detection by management or other customers. Even if they sit in their car outside the wireless hotspot they are fearful of being discovered as they view pornography or masturbate. I believe this lack of privacy is the reason most law enforcement fears have not been realized when it comes to wireless technology and child exploitation crimes.

Wi-Fi in the form of a wireless router used in your home is also a popular way to have more than one computer at home online at the same time. These routers allow the computer to connect via cable or through Wi-Fi technology. The downside to this technology is that most people bring the wireless router home, take it out of the box, plug it in and connect. These routers have the capability of broadcasting the connection signal for 800 to 1000 feet. In most neighborhoods that means many of your neighbors can also see the signal from your router and connect using your account, and this leaves you vulnerable to freeloaders surfing the internet while you pay for the connection. Before using a wireless router, read the directions for changing the **default settings** of the router. Change the name of the **service set identifier** or **SSID**. I personally use a Linksys wireless router. The default SSID is "Linksys" and if I bring the router home and plug it in, it will broadcast the name "Linksys" to my neighborhood and basically invite all my neighbors to connect to my router. To make it more difficult for others to connect to my router I need to change some of the default settings. First, change the name of the SSID and turn off the broadcasting of the SSID. Next, set an encryption key or password that will be exchanged when the computer asks the router for a connection. If the correct key is not exchanged between the computer and the router, the connection will not be allowed. There are other settings that can be changed to further limit the access, but I do not want to get too technical. **Personal Favorite: Linksys** because of the ease of connecting and the customer service support. I have called the support line and found them to be a great resource for fixing the mistakes I made when changing some of the default settings. Do not let this scare you, changing the default settings is not that difficult and must be done to secure your internet connection from intruders.

V. Virus Protection and Updates

One last piece of software was necessary for my nephew's computer: an antivirus program. There are several reputable antivirus programs available; see which one you like most. I have used several; in fact, there are different programs installed on my personal computers and my work computers, and they both work well. Some internet service providers (sometimes called an "ISP") now include antivirus programs as a standard feature for online accounts. There are a lot to choose from, but my **Personal Favorite** is **McAfee SecurityCenter**. I have this installed on my home computer and personal laptop. McAfee SecurityCenter combines Virus Scan, Personal Firewall, SiteAdvisor and Spam Blocker to help protect my computers. I prefer the interface of SecurityCenter and the update features and notifications of McAfee's programs over the others. The main reason I like McAfee is the ease of use and understanding, as well as the notifications. These are qualities to consider when choosing an antivirus program.

Most people buy a computer and are told they have a free trial of the antivirus program or they install an antivirus program and forget about it. They think it will automatically update and be ready for any virus or Trojan. However, the truth is you need to configure your software to update on a regular basis. I found McAfee's configuration easy to set up and update.

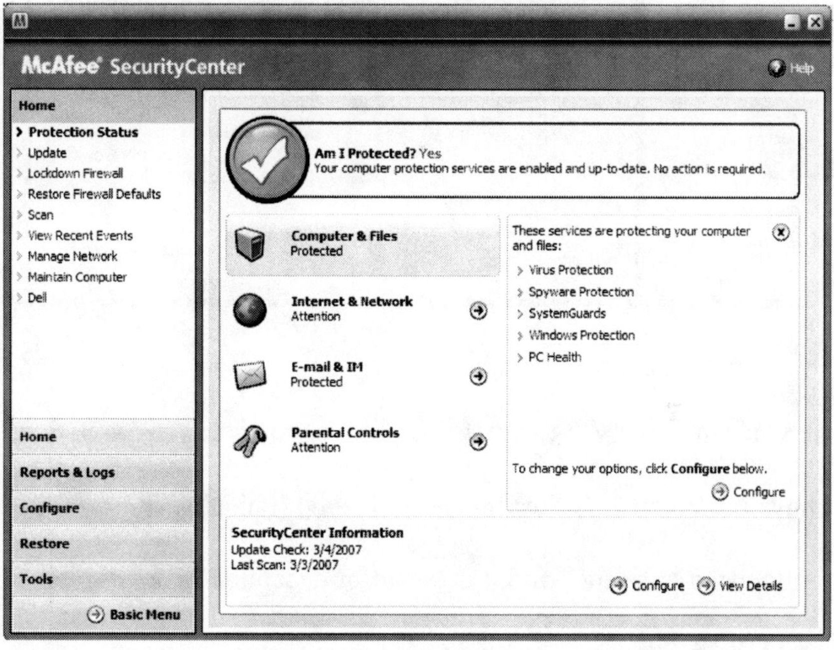

The program divides up the different areas of protection and allows me to set the level of protection for the computer and files on the computer. This is real-time protection and it has a simple notification when a possible problem is identified.

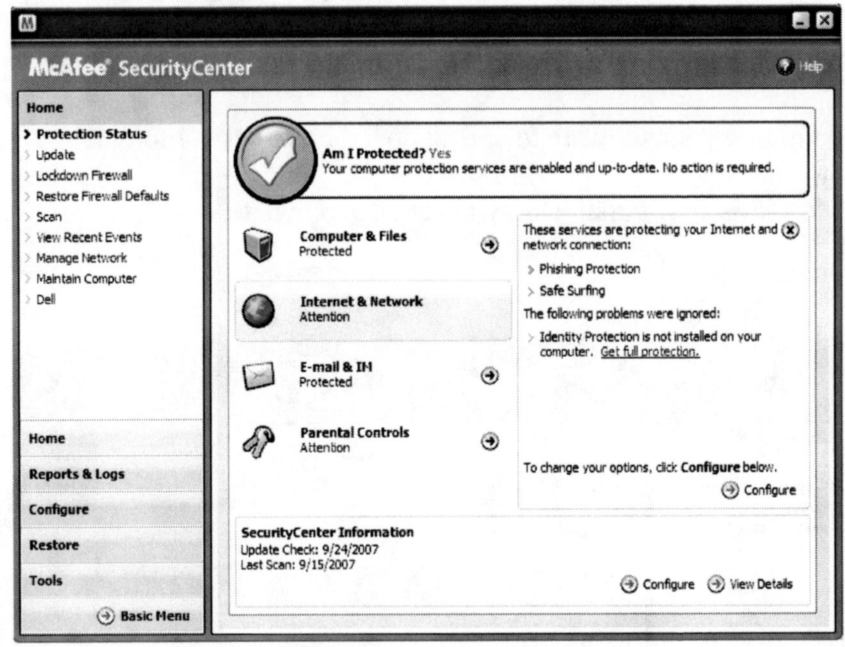

As you can see, my *Internet & Network* is requesting my attention. I have turned on *Safe Surfing* and *Phishing*. (Phishing is pronounced "fishing," and it is the art of deception in the digital world. In most cases, phishing is designed to deceive an unknowing victim in order to steal their identity or ultimately their money. Almost everyone has heard of the phishing scam in which you receive an email explaining that a millionaire in a foreign country is about to lose all his money due to a corrupt government seizing his funds. If you would be kind enough to allow the millionaire to deposit his money in your account, just until he can legally open an account in your country, he will allow you to keep any interest earned on his millions of dollars. Common sense should take hold here. What millionaire is unable to open a bank account anywhere they want? This scam has changed a little and now you may receive an email letting you know you are to receive payment from an estate that is being settled. Both scams have the same purpose, to get you to supply your bank account information so they can put the funds from the millionaire or the settlement into your account. However, once you supply the account information your bank account is drained.) I opted not to use the *Identity Protection*. My *E-mail & IM* (instant messaging) is protected, but the *Parental Controls* are requesting attention.

I did not install the content blocking feature offered as parental controls. I prefer another program, a **Personal Favorite** by **Cyber Sentinel**, as a parental control. When it comes to parental controls there are basically two types: blocking or filtering. I personally think the filtering method works better than blocking, but I am getting ahead of myself. Later on I will explain parental controls in more detail and give some pointers on how to choose the right one for your family.

The most common way for a hacker to exploit your computer is through a "hole" in your software. This means that some of the software you use may have flaws that are not noticed when it is released, but after being on the market for a period of time these flaws or "holes" are discovered. Most companies create "patches" to fix the "holes" and in most cases they are made available for free download. Probably the most common are **updates** for the Windows operating system. Every now and then your computer notifies you that there are updates available for your operating system. The computer can reach out via the internet for the update and install it automatically, but only if the Automatic Updates feature is turned on. For Windows users, turning on the Automatic Updates feature is probably the single most important way to keep your home computer safe. Think of it this way: If every so often someone published a notification of a deficiency in an alarm protecting a bank, don't you think a burglar would read about those deficiencies and use them to enter the bank and steal the money? This is how hackers can learn of deficiencies discovered in your software, and if you have not downloaded and installed the patch they can exploit the deficiency to attack your computer and view or steal your personal information.

Turning on the Automatic Updates is simple. Left click on the start button and navigate to the *Control Panel* on the menu.

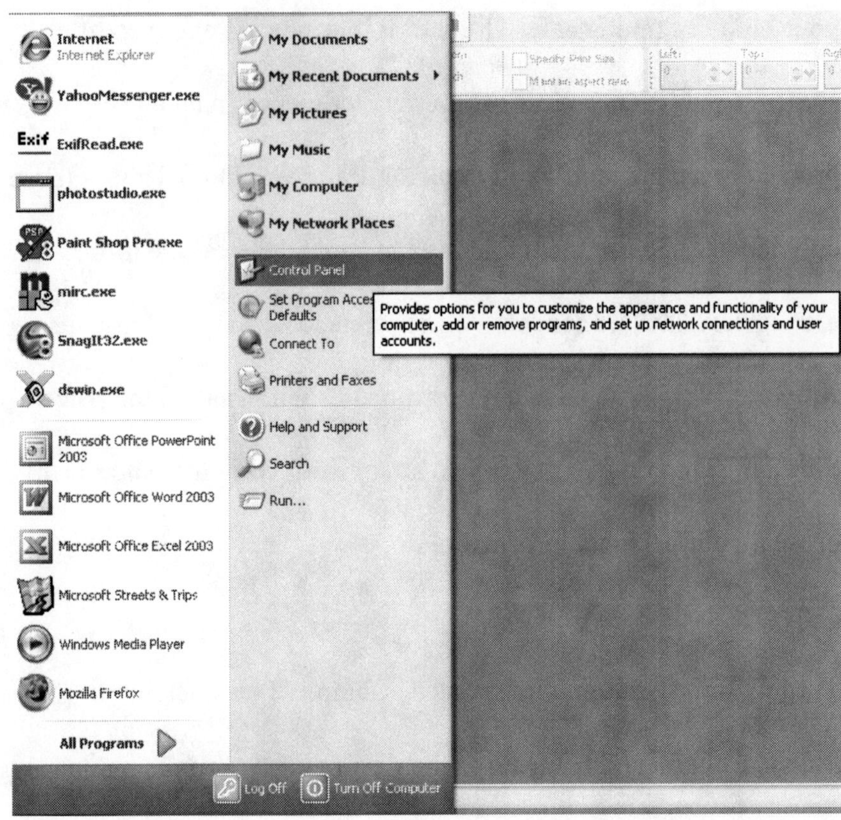

Once you click on the *Control Panel* you will see the button for the *Security Center*. This is the category view:

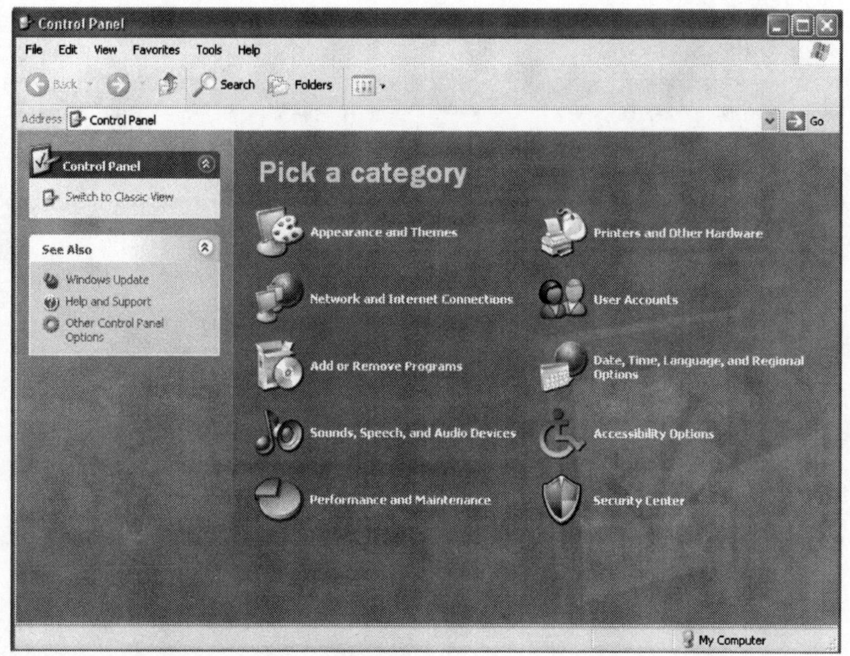

Click on the *Security Center* icon.

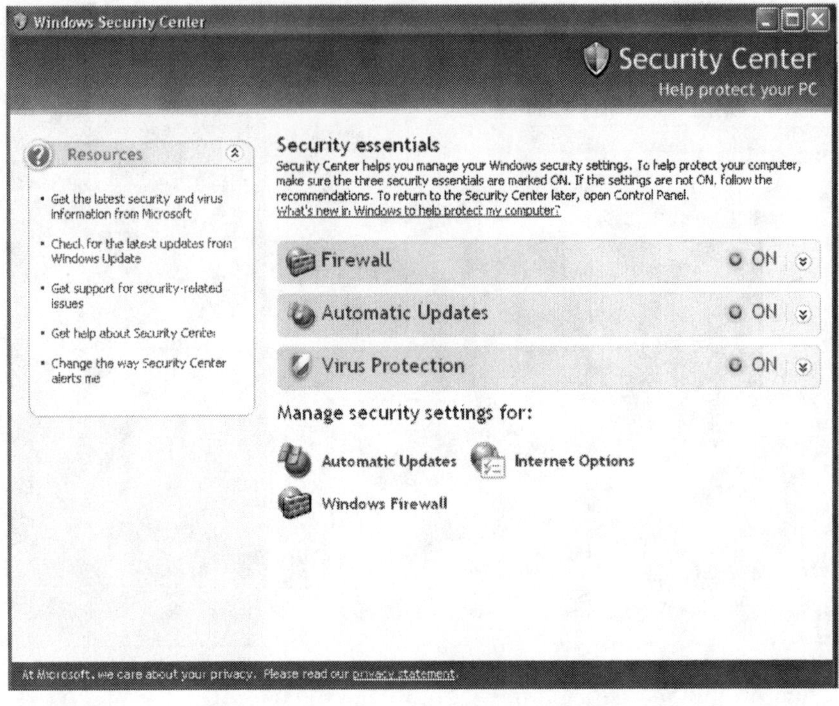

In the *Security Center* window you will see the settings for the *Windows Firewall*, *Automatic Updates* and *Virus Protection*. Click on the *Automatic Updates* button at the bottom of the window, just above the *Windows Firewall* button.

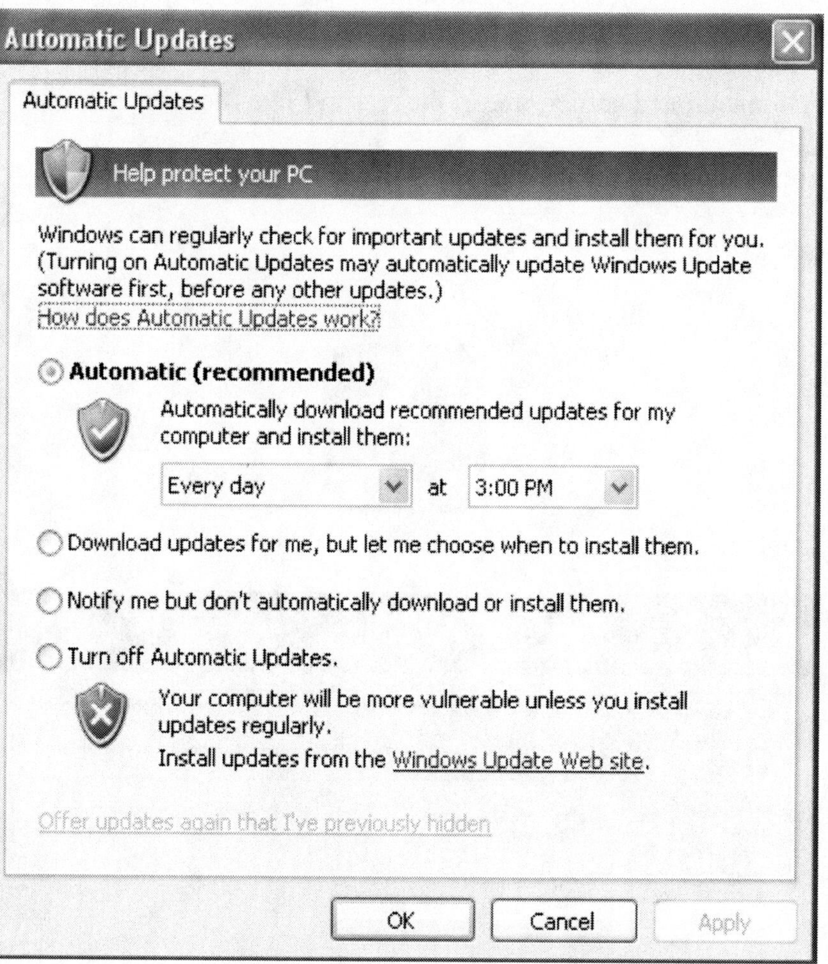

Select the time when you want the Automatic Updates to run. Remember to select a time when the computer will be turned on and connected to the internet. This process sometimes can cause a lag in other programs running on the computer so you might not want to pick the peak time for homework. Have the updates run prior to or after peak computer usage.

As I mentioned earlier, one of the reason I like McAfee is its notifications. In the taskbar you will see the icon for the SecurityCenter:

Double click this icon to see the status of the computer.

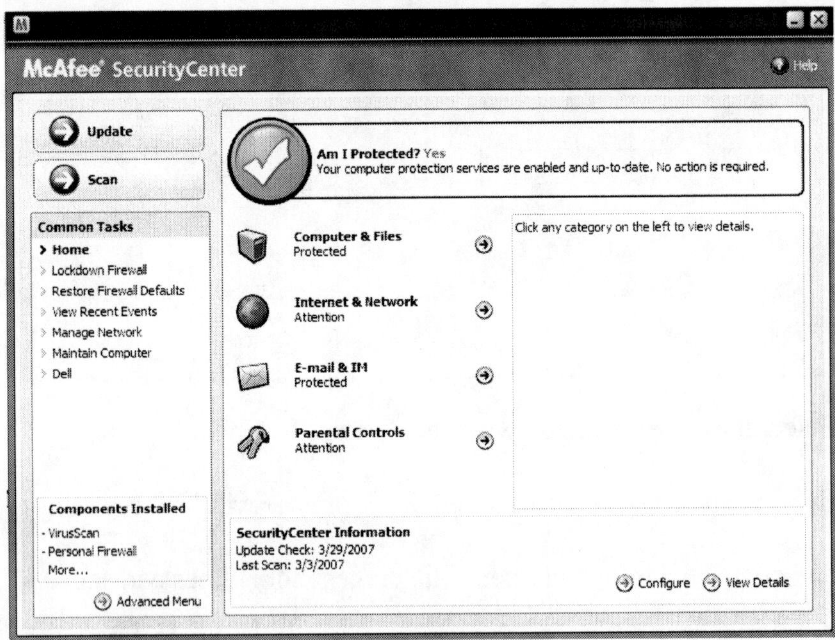

In the upper left corner of the interface is the *Update* button. Clicking on the *Update* button tells the software to check for any new updates and to automatically install them. It is important to update regularly, especially if the computer has been offline for a period of time. It is also a good idea to check for any updates before checking email or beginning to surf the internet. However, like the *Windows Updates*, there is an *Automatic Updates* setting. If the program is checking and updating, an icon that looks like this will appear:

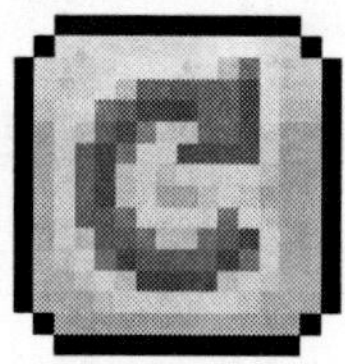

I like the interactive method of the arrow circling to let me know the program is actually running and updating. If it were to run and update without any notification it would leave me wondering if the program was actually working.

To make sure the *Automatic Updates* in the *SecurityCenter* are turned on, double click on this icon:

Then click on the *Configure* button. Click on the arrows to open the *Automatic Updates* section and make sure the *On* button is marked.

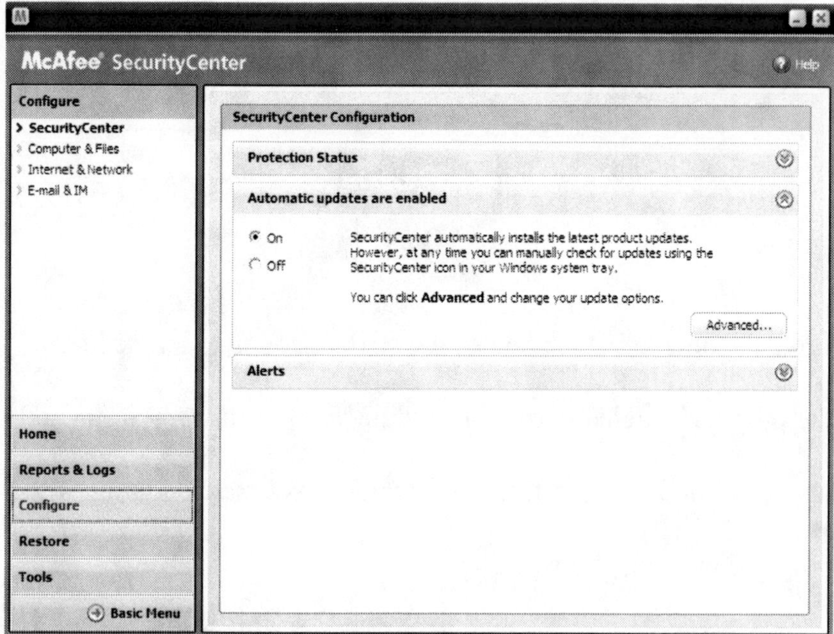

If you want to see what options have been set for the *Automatic Updates*, click on the *Advanced* button.

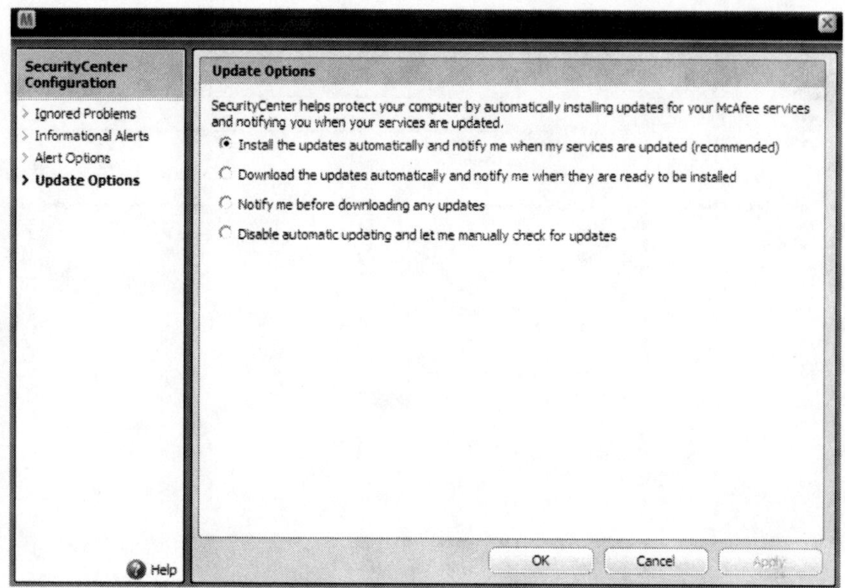

As you can see, I prefer to be notified that the program has been updated. You can pick the setting you like best.

The program will automatically run scans of your computer to see if any spyware, Trojan or virus has made its way onto your computer. After the scan is complete, you can view a report of what actions the program has taken to protect your computer.

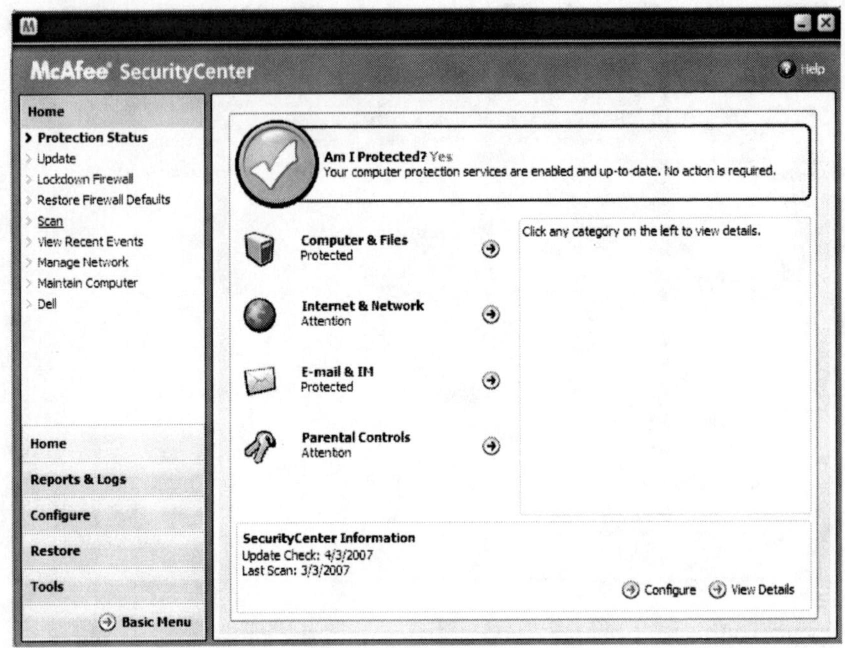

Click on *Scan* to see the details of what the scan was looking for, where it looked and what the scan found.

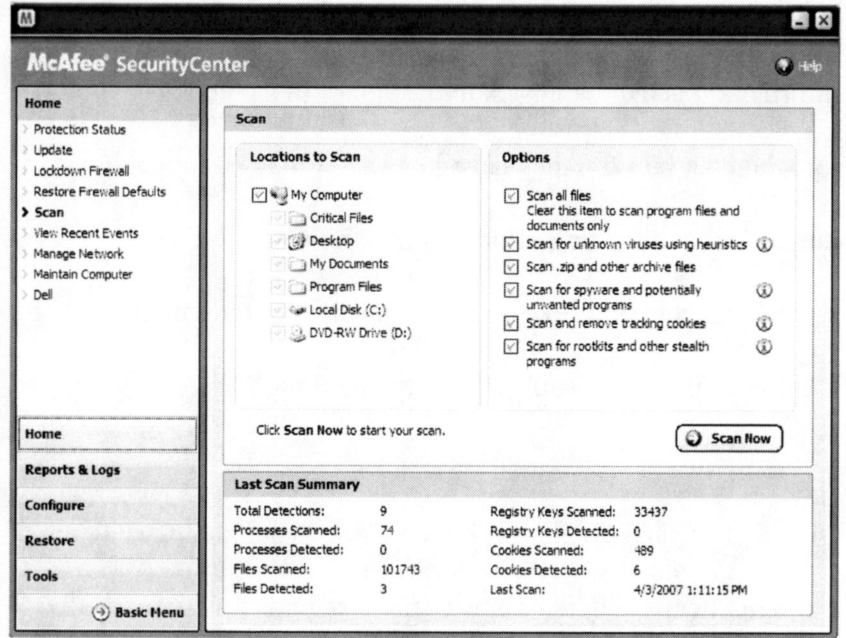

In this case it found six suspicious cookies. What is a *cookie*? A cookie is a file that resides on your computer and usually holds some information about your surfing habits or sites you have visited. Are cookies good or bad? The answer is both. Some cookies serve a useful purpose. Say you have visited and joined a site. In this case, the cookie can hold some of the information you submitted to the site when you joined. The next time you connect to the site it gathers the information stored in the cookie, says hello to you by your name and lets you enter the site. In this case it can be useful. In other circumstances the cookie may track where you visit, what type of sites you visit and what you view. This information is then sent back to the author of the cookie and used for whatever purpose they have in mind. It may be something as iniquitous as marketing information on how you shop, or it may be something dangerous like gathering personal information. Obviously the latter would be a very bad thing.

Now that you have a general knowledge of your computer, some of its components, and how some of the programs function, let's move on. In the next chapter we will look at what programs your child might have installed on your computer and what might help you to protect your children.

CHAPTER 2: PARENTAL CONTROL

I. How Do I Know What Programs My Child Has Installed?

This is probably the question I hear most often from parents at Internet Safety Presentations. The answer is to look at the list of programs installed on your computer. To make sure a computer-literate child has not hidden some of the programs, you need to look in several different areas of your computer. The first place to look is in the list of programs displayed from the *Start* button. Left click on the *Start* button and then either click on or hover over All Programs ▷ and a list of programs installed on your computer will appear. It will look something like this:

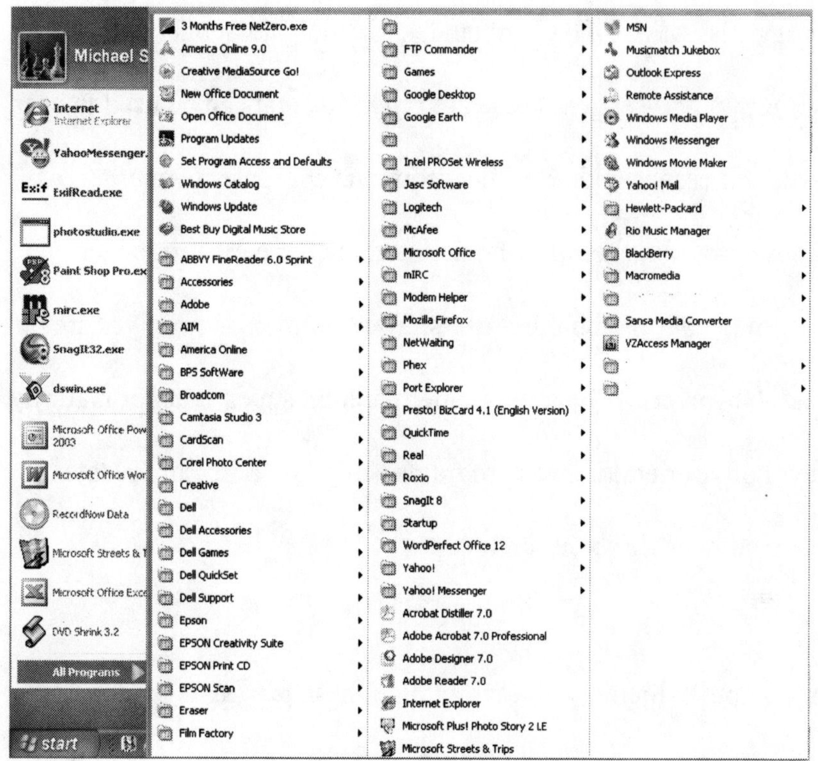

You can read the list of programs to see what has been installed on your computer. Some of the programs like America Online, Microsoft Office and McAfee may have been installed when your computer was manufactured. If you selected certain software packages they were pre-loaded onto the computer for all use by all users. These are not necessarily the programs that are of concern to parents. Most parents are looking for programs that allow their children to access the internet and interact with other people, including strangers. On this list you would be concerned with the programs: AIM, FTP Commander, Yahoo! Messenger and Windows Messenger. These are programs that can be used to chat, instant message and send files from one computer to another. These programs use your home internet connection to launch communication with other users. The programs themselves are not bad. However, without the proper parental supervision or maturity level of your child, these programs can allow a sexual predator to have contact with your child.

A computer-literate child might hide these programs by deleting the shortcut from the list of *All Programs*. What you see on the list of *All Programs* is just a shortcut to the executable file that launches the program from your hard drive. The shortcut can be deleted without deleting the actual program.

In this example the shortcut for the Rio Music Manager appears in the *All Programs* list.

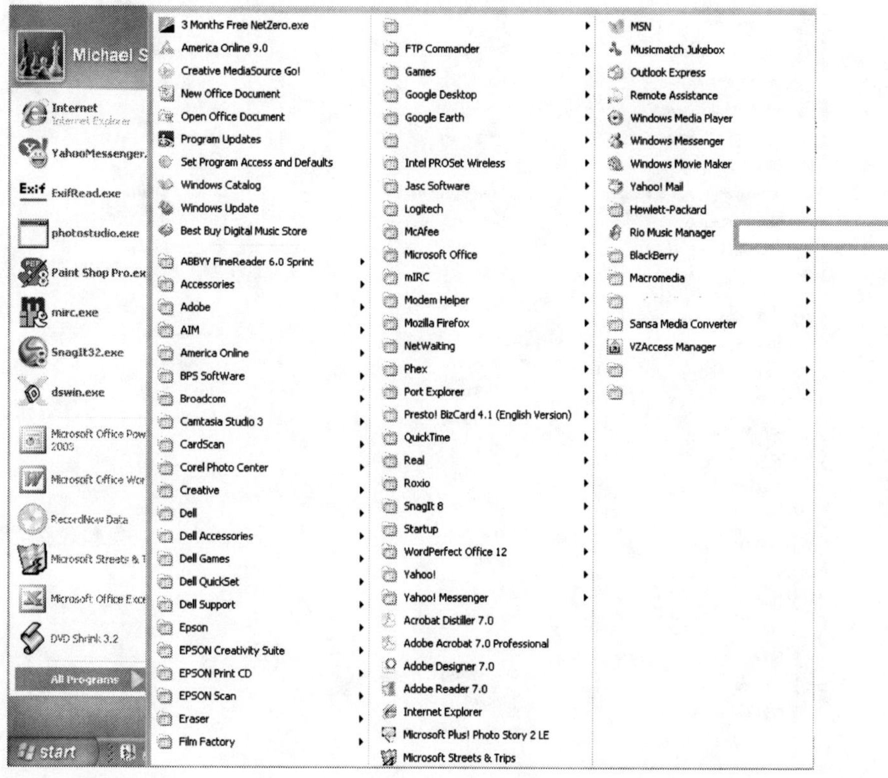

Your child can simply right click on the shortcut and select the *Delete* option.

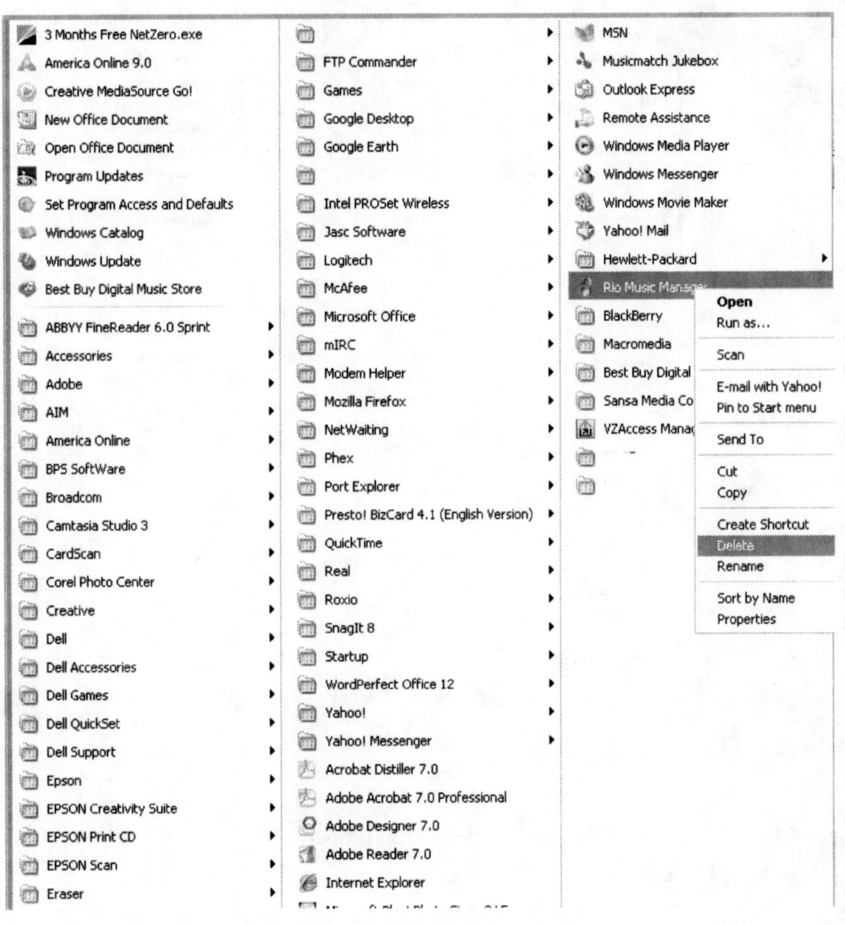

Clicking on the *Delete* option will cause the computer to display a warning screen.

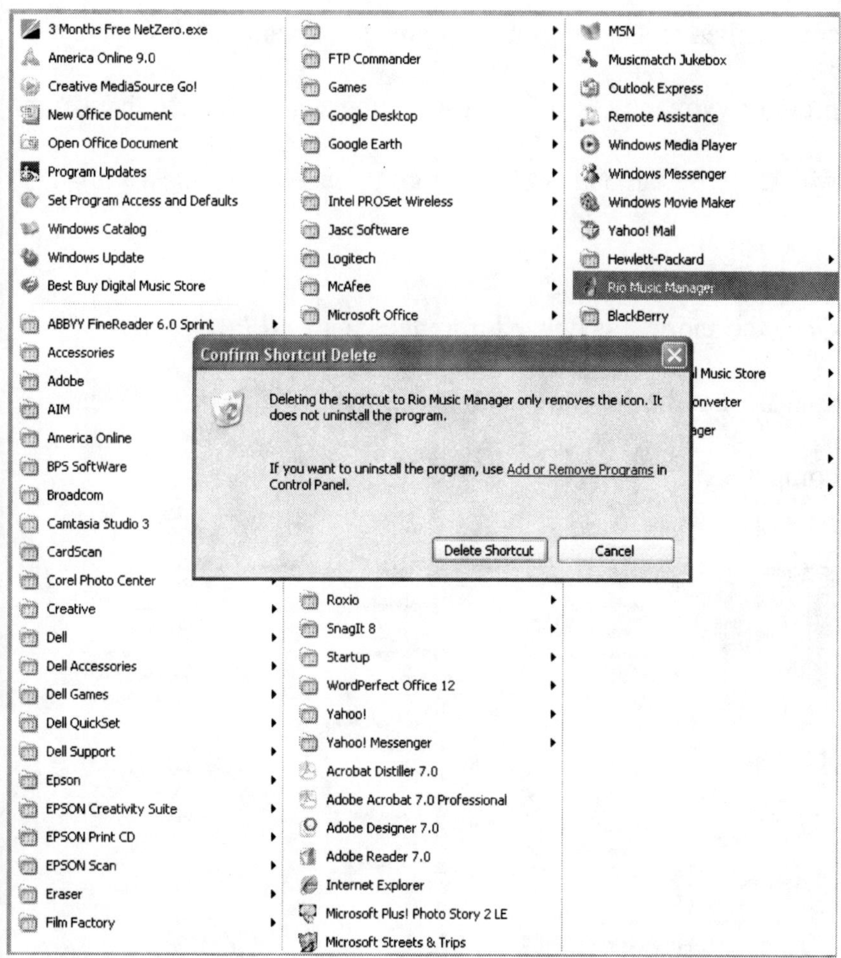

The warning is letting you know that this action will only delete or remove the shortcut from the *All Programs* list and does not uninstall the actual program. If you want to uninstall the program you would have to use the *Add or Remove Programs* feature in the *Control Panel*. Later in this chapter I will explain the procedure for using the *Add or Remove Programs* feature to see what programs are installed and to uninstall any you don't want. With some programs you may be able to use an uninstall command that comes with the program and not have to go through the *Control Panel*.

Once the shortcut is deleted from the list of *All Programs*, it appears that the program is no longer available for use on this computer.

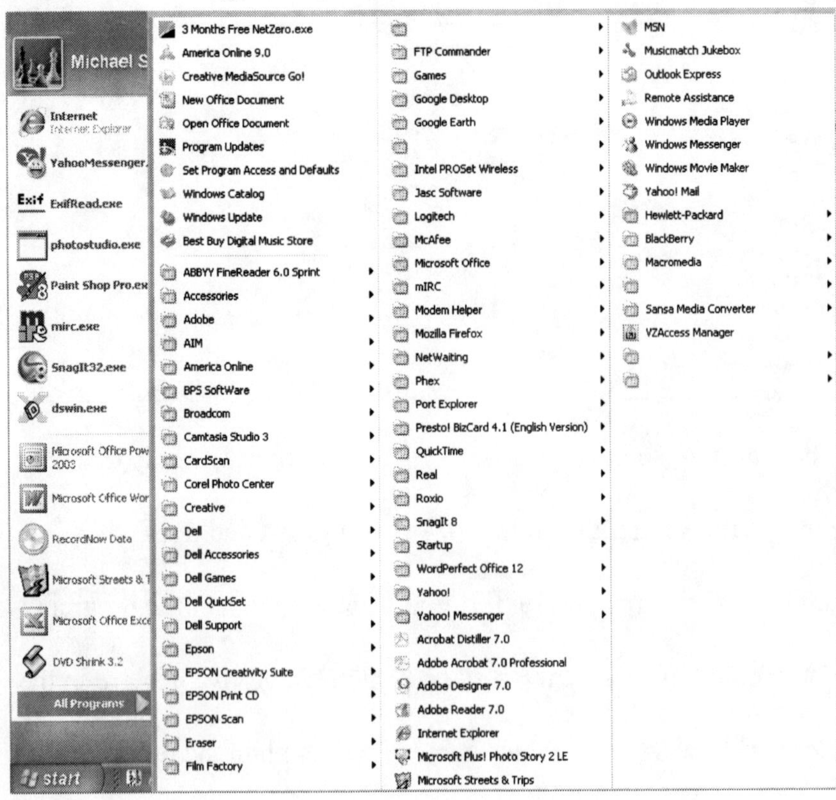

However, if we look at the hard drive via Windows Explore we may find the program. To look for the program using Windows Explore, right click on *Start* and then left click on *Explore*.

This will open up Windows Explore and allow you to see items saved to your hard drive or other storage devices if they are attached to your computer. Other storage devices could be compact disc (CD), Digital Versatile Disc or Digital Video Disc (DVD), an additional internal or external hard drive or other storage formats like a memory card or flash drive. In this example we are looking for program files installed by our children so we will navigate to the *Program Files* subdirectory in on the computer's hard drive.

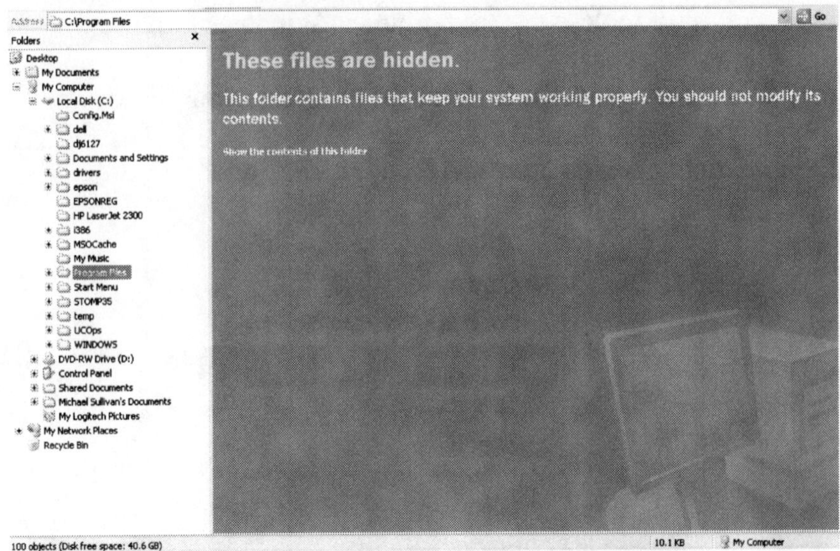

The first time you visit the list of *Program Files* you may receive a warning message that this folder or subdirectory contains files that keep your computer working properly. Since our goal here is just to view the list and not delete any of the files, it is safe to click on the *Show the contents of this folder* link.

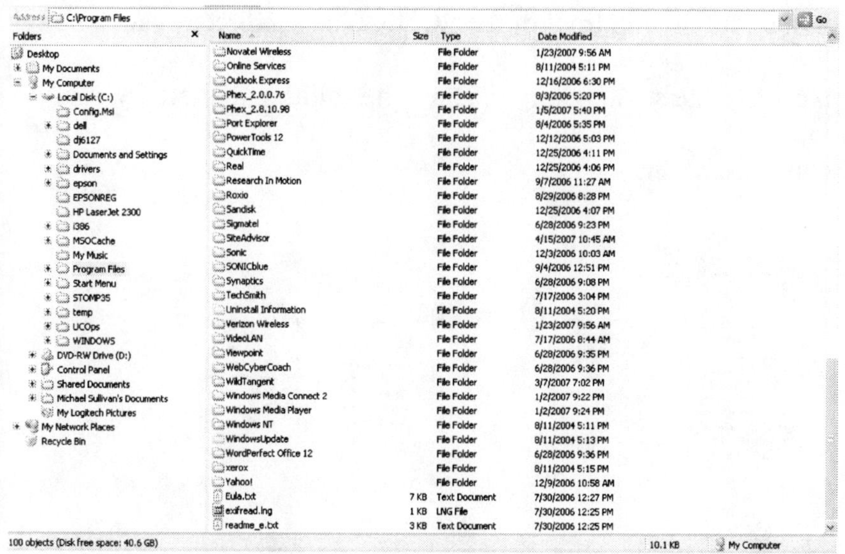

In this view, the programs installed to the C: drive in the subdirectory named *Program Files* will appear in the right hand window. This does not mean these are the only programs installed on your computer. Programs can be installed in any location on the hard drive. You can also look through the subdirectories under *My Computer*.

However, by default the bulk of the programs your children use to chat, instant message or transfer files should be found in the *Program Files* subdirectory. In this example we deleted the Rio Music Manager shortcut from the *All Programs* list. Since the Rio Music Manager is part of the SONICblue program I have clicked on the plus sign in front of the SONICblue subdirectory and expanded the subdirectory to show the additional directory of Rio Music Manager.

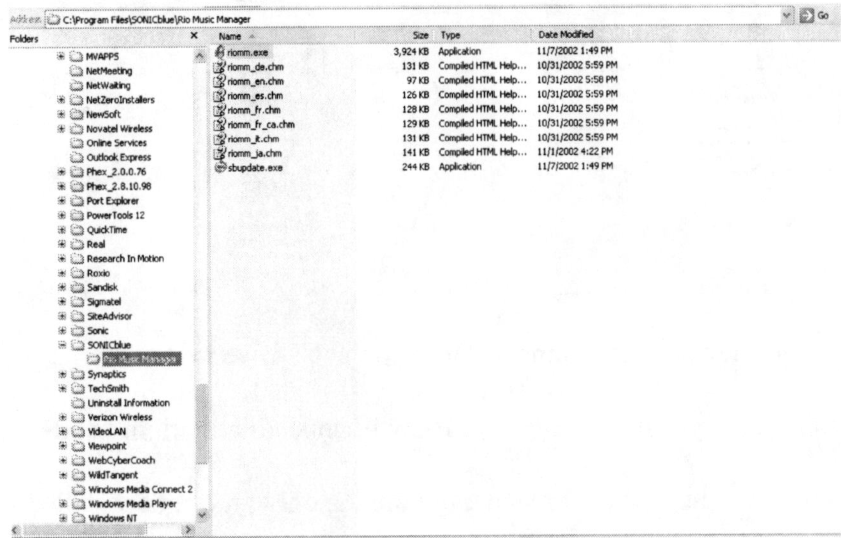

As you can see, the executable (the file ending with the ".exe" extension) for launching Rio Music Manager is still on the hard drive, located under the subdirectories of SONICblue and Rio Music Manager. If I were to double click the *riomm.exe* icon, it would open the program and allow me to edit the music stored on my MP3 player (an MP3 player is portable personal music or video player).

As I mentioned earlier, another way to see what programs have been installed is to click on the *Start* button, then click on *Control Panel* and finally on *Add or Remove Programs*.

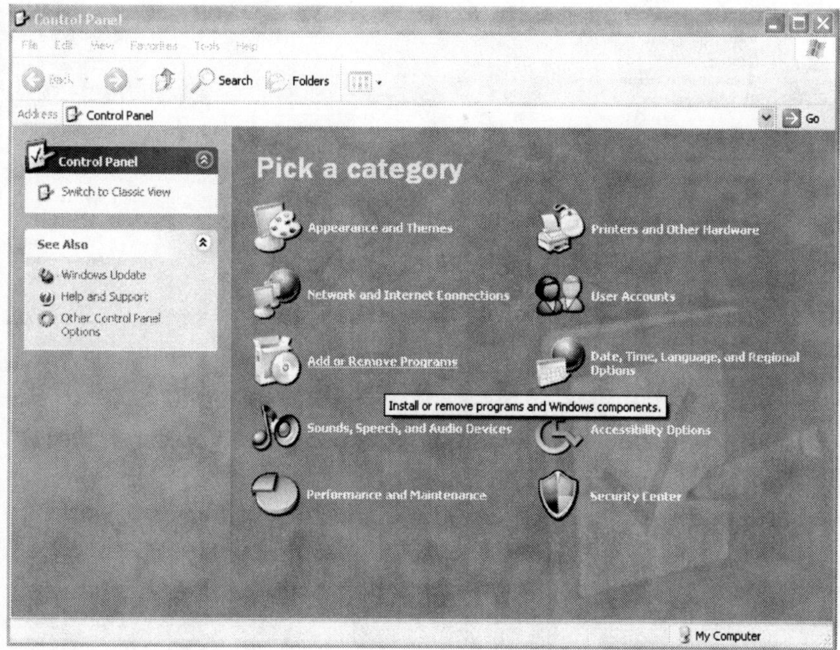

You will see a list of programs installed on your computer. You may have to give it a few seconds to populate the list.

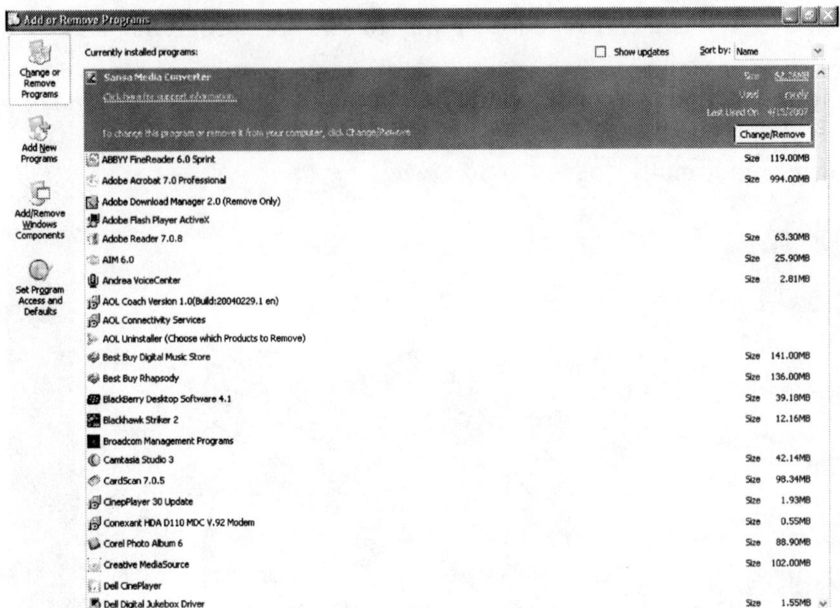

If you see one you do not want on your computer you can remove the program with just a few mouse clicks. *Be careful here; make sure you are removing an unwanted program and not one that is vital to the operation of your computer.* If you find a program on the computer that you do not recognize, try typing the name of the program into a search engine such as Google (www.google.com).

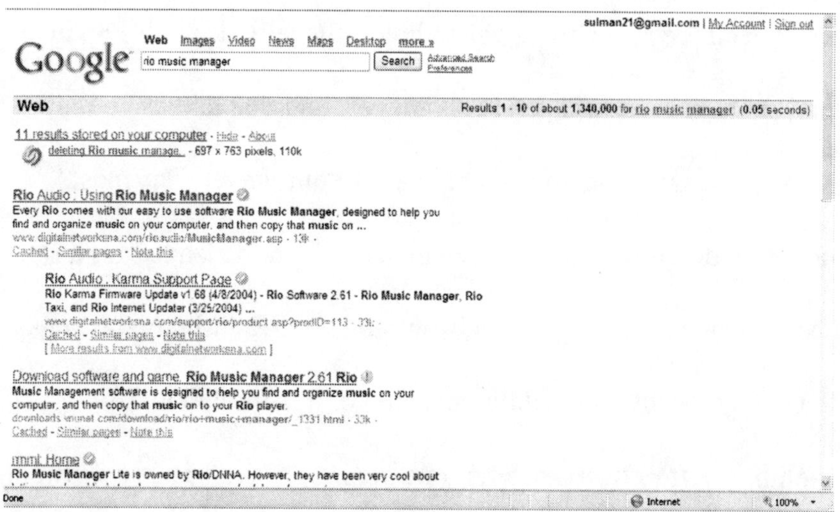

In this example, the results let you know that Rio Music Manager is a free software package that comes with every Rio MP3 player. It is used to find and organize music files on your computer and transfer the files to the Rio MP3 player. This is not a program that would be used to chat or instant message so it is not one to be concerned about for online predators. However, you may want to make sure your child is not illegally downloading copyrighted materials such as music or movies. Most children and some parents can be easily confused about this issue. The most commonly heard questions are, "If I use a free program am I violating the law, and if the programs are illegal why are they so widely available?" The simple rule to follow is if you are not paying a fee to download music you are probably downloading it illegally. Most MP3/video players have an associated software program that allows you to sign up to legally download content for your player. The most common downloads are songs which can be downloaded for a set fee. This fee is usually a certain amount per file (usually this runs between 50 cents and a dollar per file) or a monthly fee. If it is monthly charge, you pay a flat rate per month and you are allowed to download content. Again, your player probably came with software that the manufacturer wants you to use to obtain the content legally. This does not mean you cannot choose one of the other legal download sites. Most players will work with content legally downloaded from other legitimate file sharing sites. Each site will supply software to download music or video content and you use the player's software to manage and transfer the content. If you are not using one of these services then most likely you or your children are downloading content illegally.

When teaching children about legal content, I try to explain how they will only be hurting themselves if they steal content. For instance, I ask them what their favorite video game is and what version they are currently using. Most of the really popular games have gone through two or three new versions. I ask them how they would feel if their favorite game never had a second or third version. Most say that they would be bored by playing the same version over and over because they have already beaten that version. I let them know that the companies that manufacture the games and the people who create the games do so not only because they enjoy creating the games, but because they are paid for their creation. If they were not paid or the companies did not make a profit from the sale of the games, they would not continue to develop new versions of the game. When software is shared illegally, no payment is received and it causes the companies to stop making the game or to stop producing new versions of the games.

Normally I ask the group of children if they ever earned an A for a grade on a test. They all raise their hands to signify that at one time or another they all got an A. I ask one of the children to tell me about the A they obtained and usually it involves studying hard for the test. I then ask them if they would be willing to share their grade with the rest of the class. In other words, even though they worked so hard to get the A, how about sharing their hard work with everyone in the class so that everyone receives an A, including the children who did not study at all? The answer from the child usually is "No! I worked hard for the grade." They know how hard they worked for that A and they do not want to share it. I then tie this into illegally sharing software and they realize how this compares to illegally obtaining music, movies and games. They now understand they were paid for their hard work by getting an A on the test. People who create the music, movies or games are paid for their hard work when the content is purchased legally.

To summarize, there a few different ways to learn what programs have been installed on your computer: the first place to look is the All Programs list, then look on the hard drive in the *Program Files* subdirectory, next look through the subdirectories under *My Computer*, and finally see what is installed on your computer using the *Add or Remove Programs* feature in the *Control Panel.* If you are unsure of the purpose of any program that is installed on your computer, google the name of the program to find information that will help you decide if the program is something you can safely remove. Be careful not to remove any software your computer needs to operate and also be aware that some perfectly legal programs can be used for illegal downloading.

II. User Accounts

Parents usually ask if there is a way to prevent their children from installing programs on the computer without the parents' knowledge. Yes, there is a simple way built into the Windows operating system that will allow a parent to take some control of the home computer and the programs installed on it. First you have to understand how user accounts work. The concept of user accounts was created in more recent versions of the Windows operating system to allow each user to sign onto a computer and have it boot up with the interface that user is most comfortable using. Some people like to have a clean desktop with very few icons showing.

This is my desktop and it has only a few icons for programs I use frequently. I prefer to go through the *Start*, *All Programs* method to launch programs. I like the neat look of only a few icons. However, I have worked with people who have an icon for every program and document they use displayed on their desktop. They have so many that they need to increase the resolution of the desktop every so often so they can see all the icons. In time they will need a magnifying glass to be able to read the names of the icons.

By setting up user accounts you can control access to files on the computer and the rights to load software. For instance, a limited user may not be able to view other users' stored documents even though they are both using the same computer and saving documents to the same hard drive. They each will have specific rights as to whether they can actually view files located in another user's subdirectories. They will also have limited rights to change the settings on the computer, which denies them the right to add programs to the computer.

It is not recommended that parents have a limited account and children have the administrator's account. To see how the user accounts are set up now, left click on *Start* and navigate to the *Control Panel*.

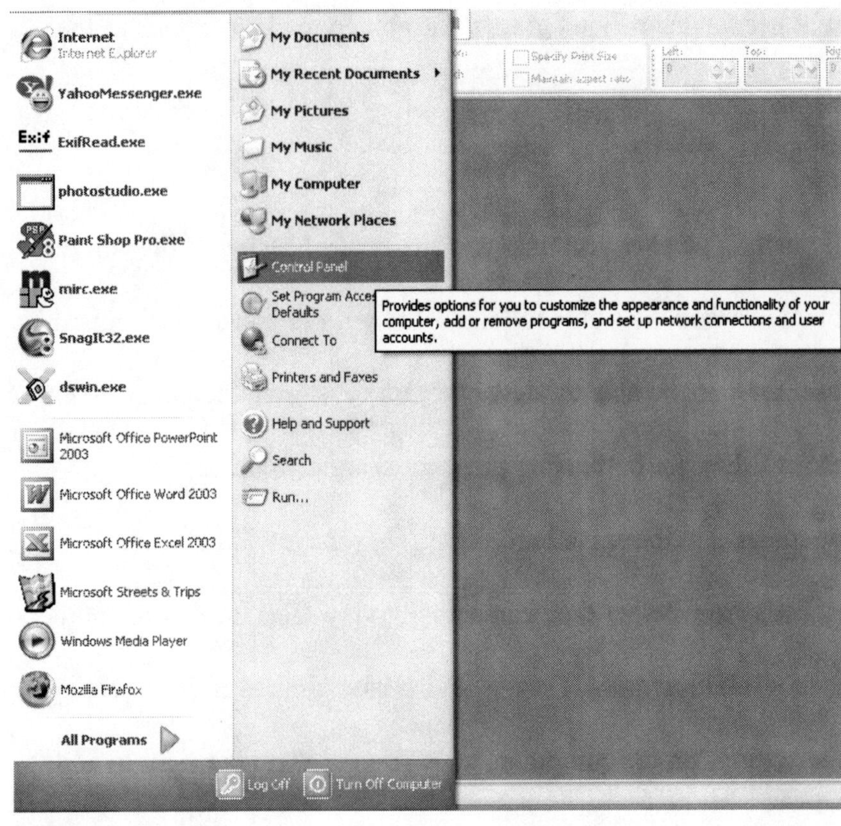

Click on *Control Panel*.

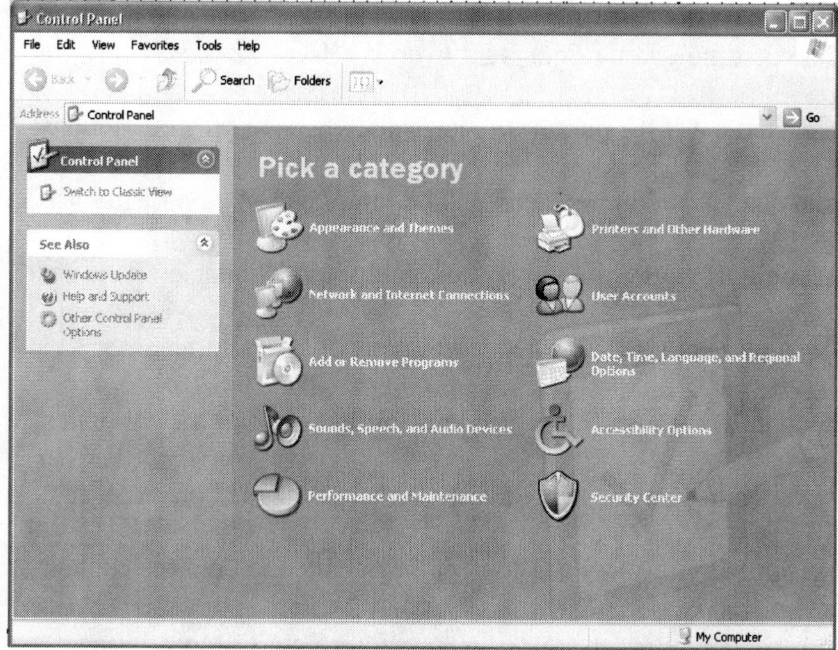

Then click on *User Accounts*.

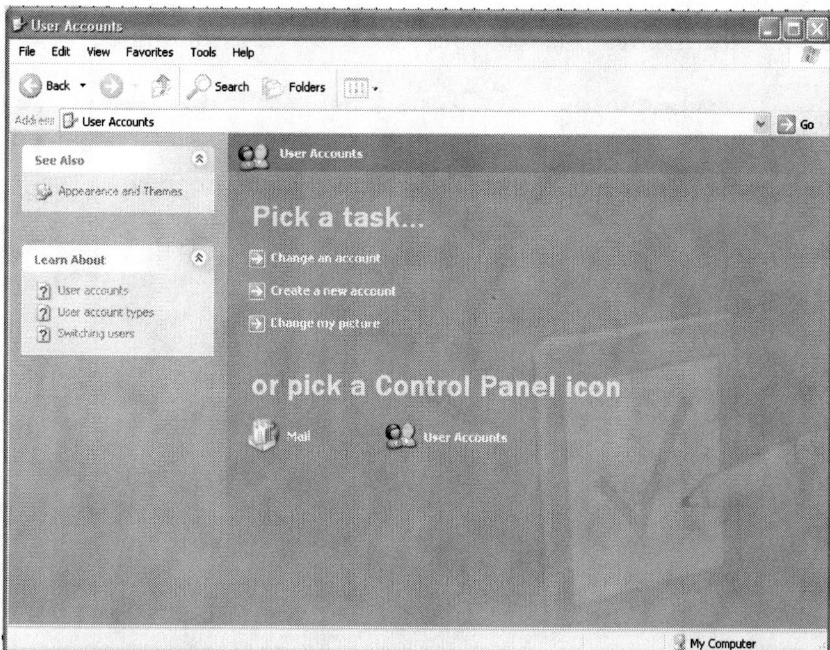

The first thing you might want to do is select *Change an account* and find out if the parameters have already been set so that mom and dad have a limited account and junior has an administrator's account. If your child is very computer literate this may have been done without your knowledge. Remember, the administrator's account allows for full access and configuration of the computer, but a limited access account allows the user signed on under that account to view only the content they created but not the content or programs of other users. It also prohibits them from installing new software or making changes to the operating system. When you are surfing the internet it is recommended that you use a limited account. This will help prevent viruses, Trojans or spyware from being able to download, install and run on your computer.

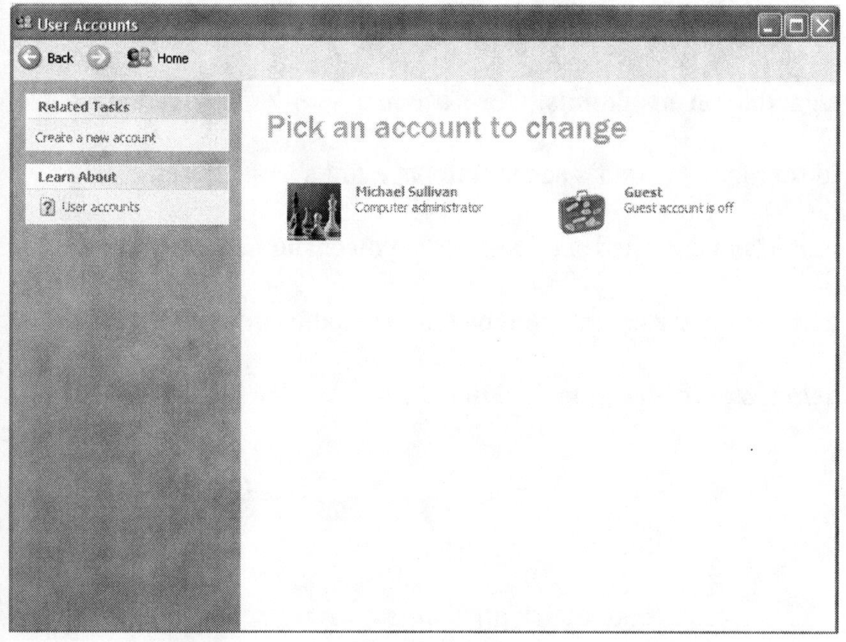

In this example, you can see the only account set up on this computer is for Michael Sullivan and it is an administrator account. This is where you need to look to see what junior did when he set up the different accounts and to find out if mom and dad's account is set to limited and junior's is set as the administrator. If there is a password you will need to use the password to access his account. Call him into the room and ask him for the password to his account in order to change the settings on everyone's accounts. Access *User Accounts* in the *Control Panel*, and change mom and dad's account to administrator status before you set junior's to a limited account. You will need to be signed in on an administrator's account in order to have the rights to set mom and dad's account to have full access. If you change junior's to a limited account before you change your own to an administrator account, you may not have the ability to access an administrator's account and make changes.

To set up an account click on *Create a new account*.

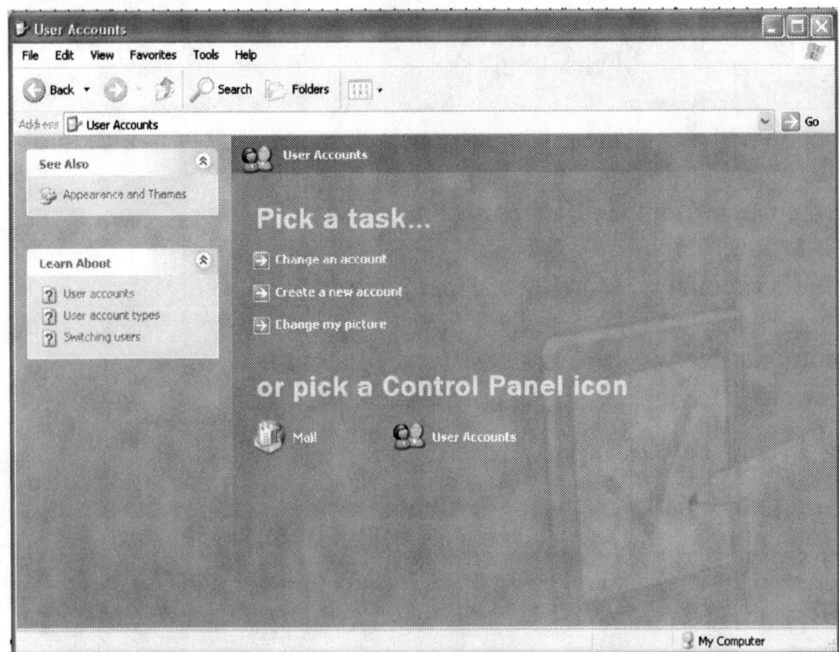

Then type in the name you want the account to have.

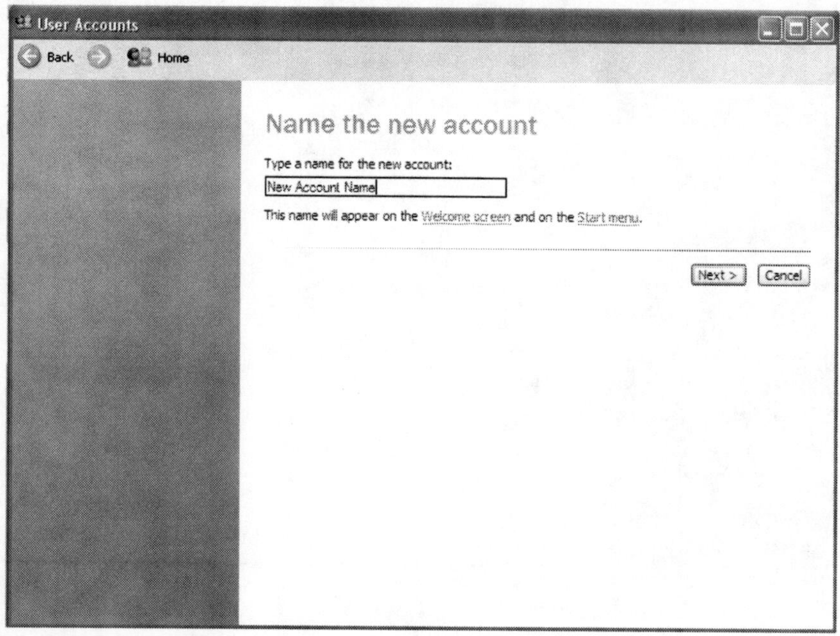

Then click on *Next* and you will be asked what type of account you want to create.

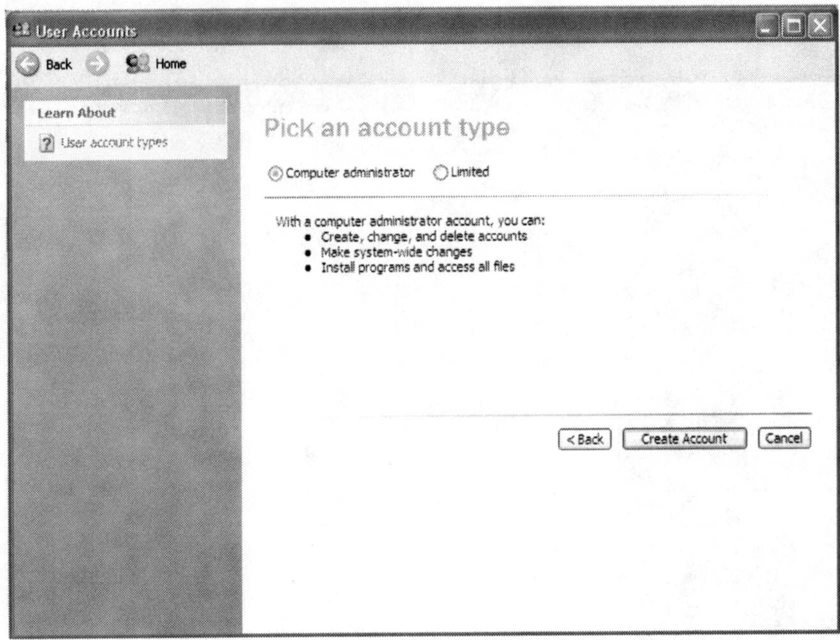

After selecting the type of account, click on *Create Account*. You will be returned to the *User Accounts* screen where each account is listed and the type of the account is displayed.

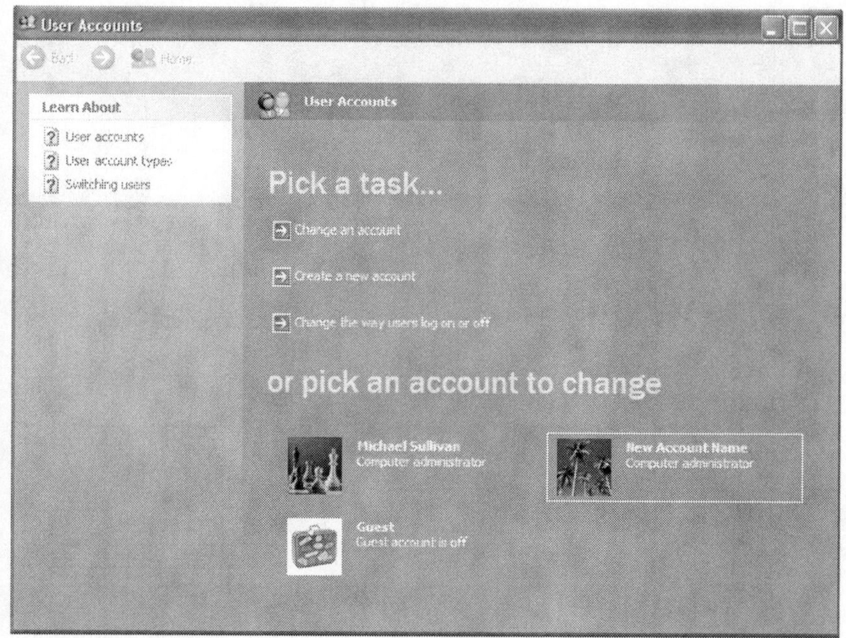

To add a password to the account, click on the name of the account to which you want to add the password and it will display several options.

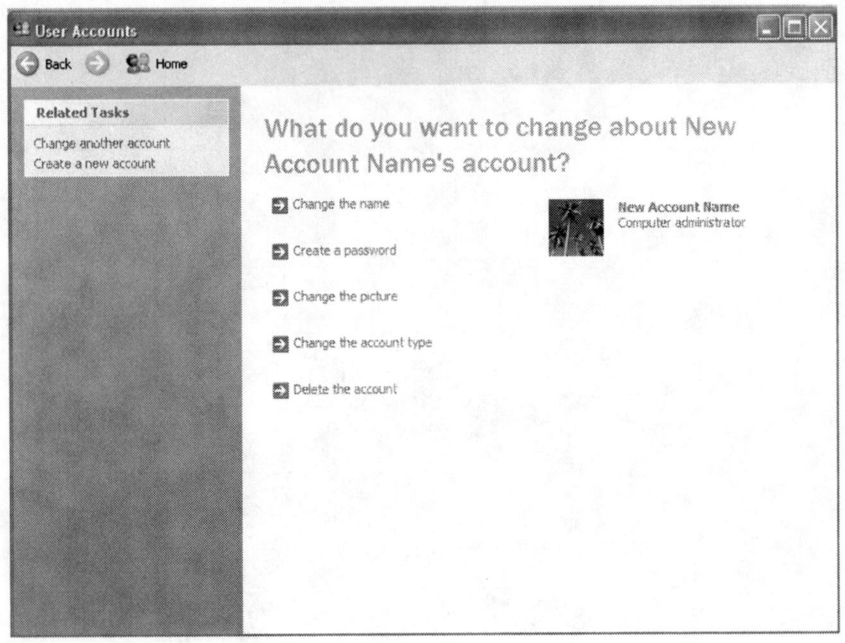

Here, you can change the user account name, create a password, change the display picture, change the account type (this is where you change junior's account back to a limited account) or delete the account. In our example, we will add a password to the account by clicking on *Create a password.*

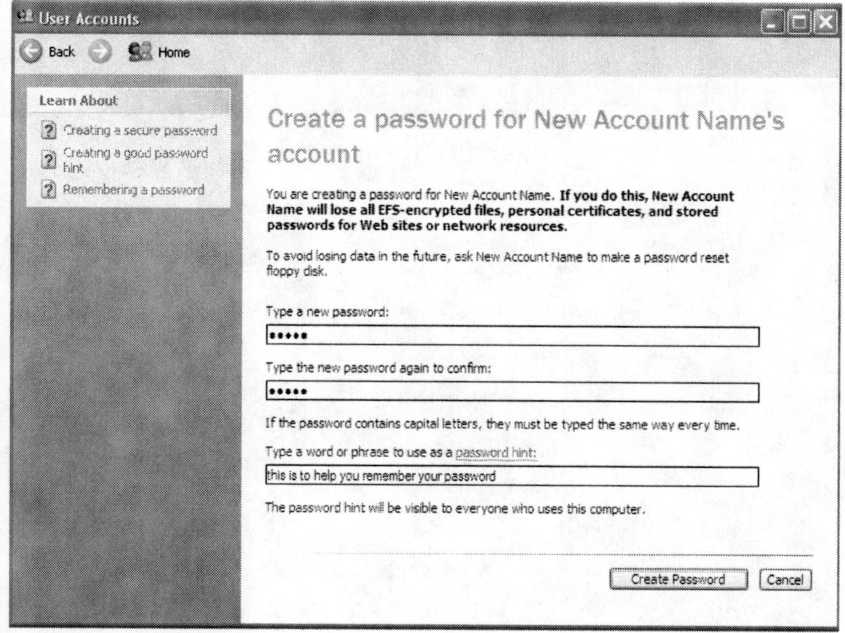

Type in your password and then retype the password to confirm.

Type in a word or phrase that will help you remember your password should you need a hint at a later date. Then click on *Create Password.*

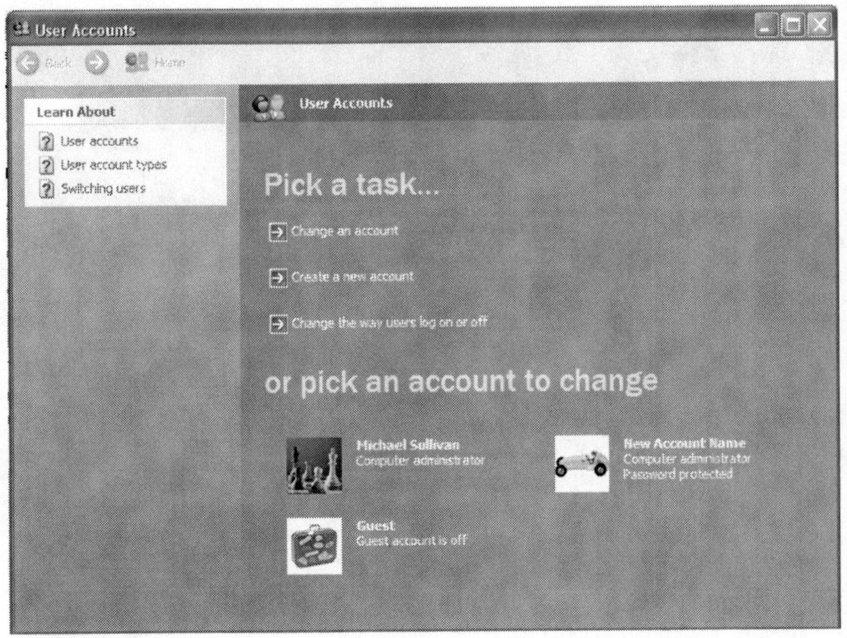

Now, remove the password from junior's account so you may access the account should the need arise. Now that you have the administrator setting and junior has the limited account, any software he wants to add to the computer will have to be done through your user account and with your approval.

III. Using Internet Explorer 7 to Filter Content

Parents usually want to know if there are settings to limit what their child can do online. There is a simple way to set the browser (Internet Explorer or Mozilla Firefox are two of the more popular browsers) to prohibit certain content from appearing. There are settings they can use to help limit the type of content displayed on their computer, but I often warn parents that there are limitations to what the free settings can and cannot prevent. I want them to understand that using these settings is a step in the right direction, but they are not the entire solution. In fact, there is no one program that will cure all the problems. But there are several settings and additional parental control programs that can be purchased and used to give parents some peace of mind that they are doing all that they can to make the internet safer for their children.

When our children are old enough to drive they go through driver's education, practice driving with their parents and take a test in order to obtain the privilege of driving a car on public streets. As parents, we make sure the car is in good working order, that it has headlights for night driving, good brakes for stopping, seatbelts, collapsible steering columns, padded dashboards and airbags in case of an accident. However, even with all these safety precautions, it cannot guarantee that anyone will survive an accident. But as parents we allow our children to venture out into the world because we have done everything possible to make it safer for our children. Using these settings and adding on parental control programs is the computer version of making sure the vehicle is as safe as possible.

I will discuss add-on parental controls a bit later, but for right now let's look at the free settings available in Internet Explorer (IE 7) and Mozilla Firefox. I use both because they each have features I like. Let's look at IE 7 first.

To find the settings, launch IE 7 and then click on *Tools* and *Internet Options*.

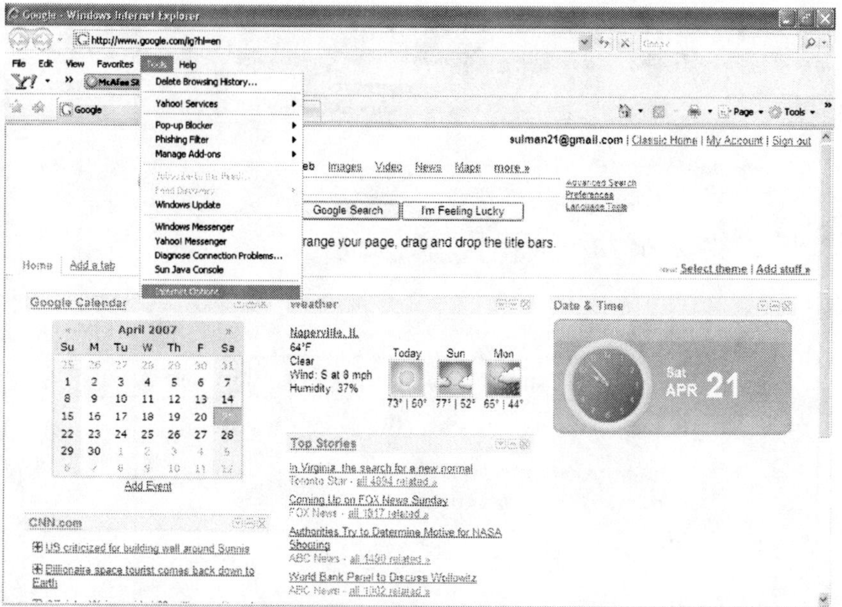

The first window that will appear will let you know what home page is set for the browser.

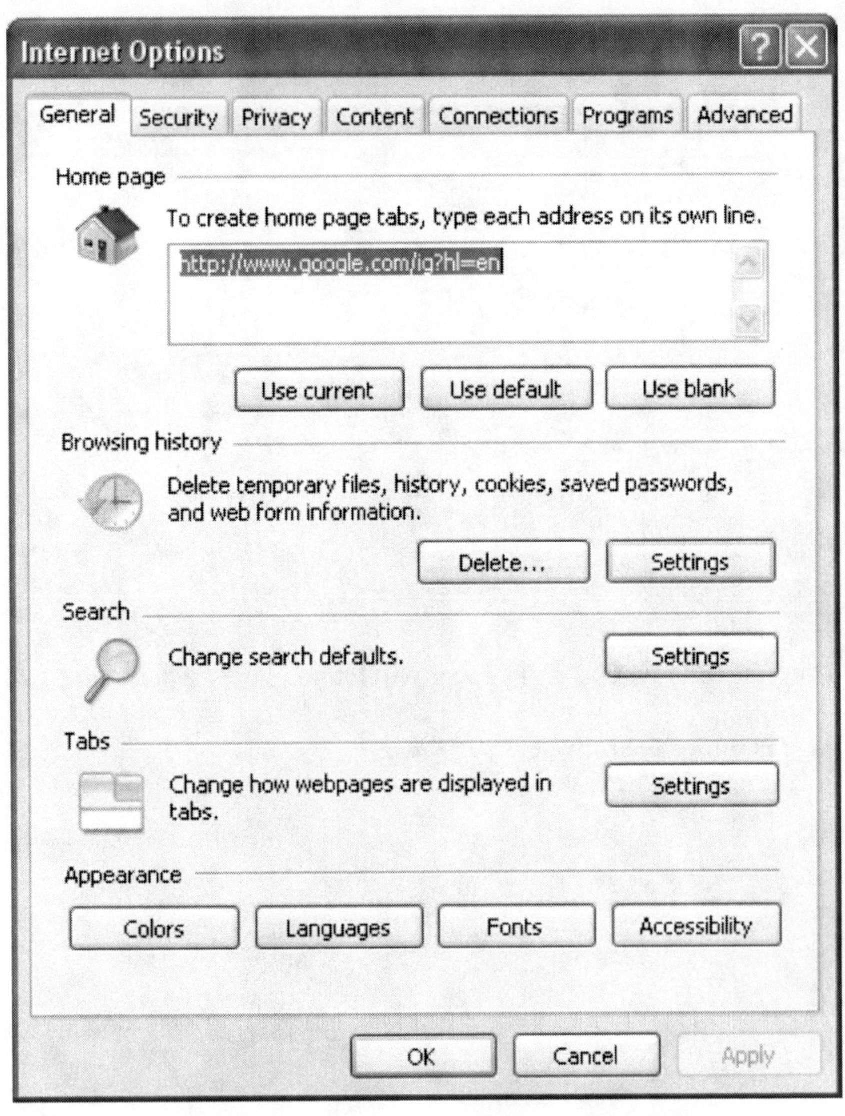

Notice that my home page is set to Google. **Personal Favorite home page: www.google.com**. I find that having a search engine as my home page saves me time. If my home page were set to launch the website for my office or my internet service provider, it would only add steps to the process of searching for information on the internet. One way to select a home page is to go to the web page first, then click on *Tools*, *Internet Options* and then click the *Use Current* button and it will pull the web address from the page currently displayed in your browser and use it for your home page. Then click on *Apply* at the lower right corner of the window and the home page will be set. The next time you launch the browser or whenever you click on the *Home* button on the browser it will go to the home page you selected.

A hint as to whether or not your child may be hiding something from you can be found by clicking on the *Settings* button under the section called *Browsing* history in the *Internet Options* screen.

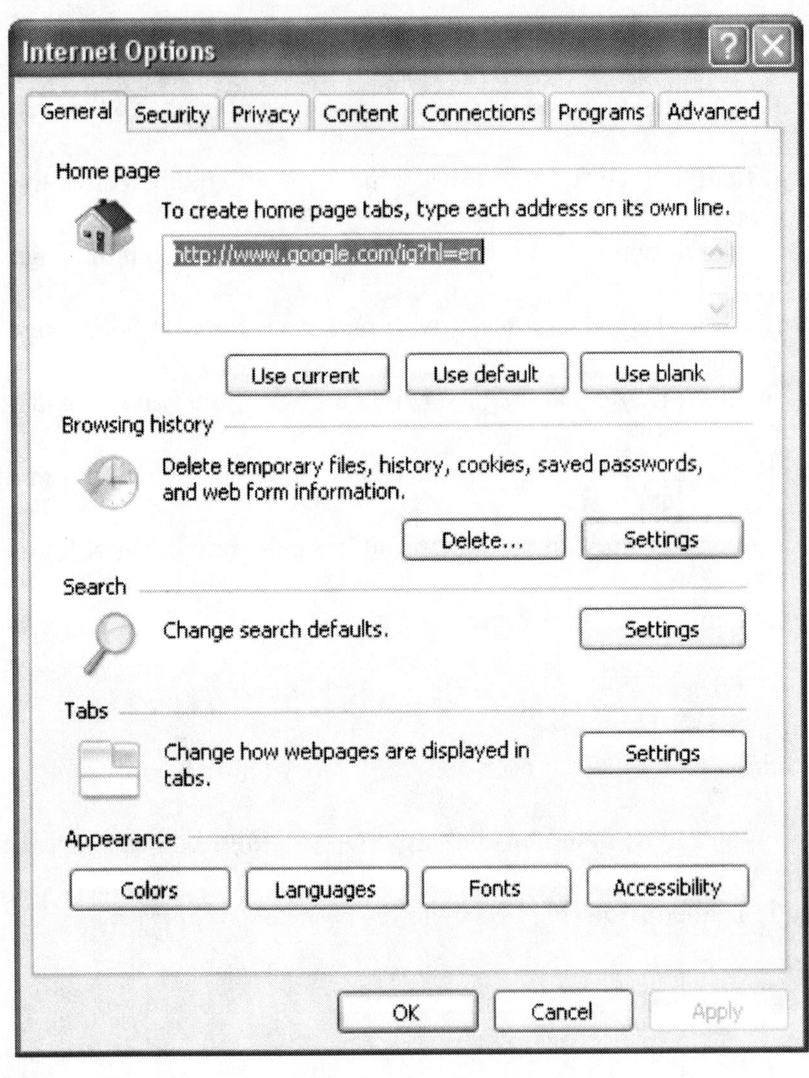

After you click on *Settings*, you will see the *Temporary Internet Files and History Settings*.

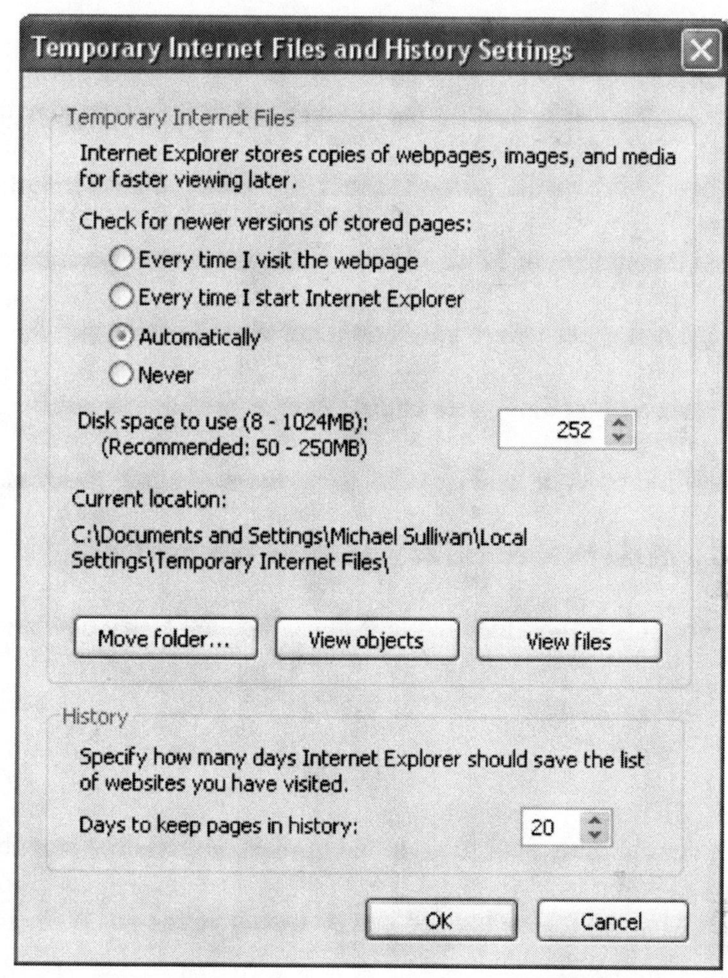

Look at the bottom of the page to see the number of days IE 7 has been set to save the list of websites visited. The default from the factory is 20 days. If this has been changed, say to zero, it is a clue that junior does not want you to know which sites he has been visiting online. Reset it to whatever number of days you want. You can make the number 20, 50 or 100 days. Set the number to a time frame that you feel you can live with. If you plan to check the history once a week, then set the number at 8 or 9 days to give a little leeway. If you are going to check the history once a month, then set the number at 32 or 33 days. This will save to your hard drive the history of where your computer visited online and the images viewed on those web pages. You do not have to worry about filling up your hard drive as these are very small thumbnail versions of the pictures and do not take up very much room. However, it is a good idea to clean these files out every now and then.

When our children want to go to the movies, responsible parents look at what the movie is rated before saying yes or no. Web pages can be rated in the same manner and you can use the browser to check the web page's rating before the page is displayed. The pages can be rated on a number of factors such as violence, intimidation, nudity, language and several other categories. To activate these controls click on *Tools*, *Internet Options* and then click on the *Content* tab.

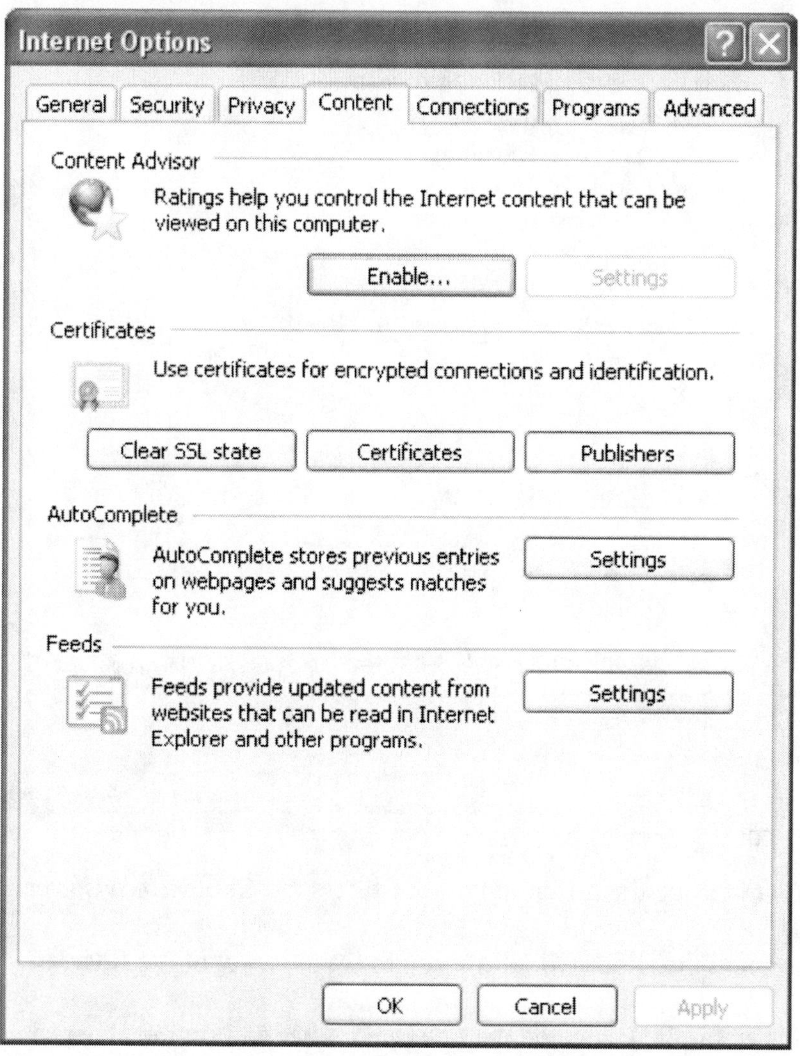

Under the *Content Advisor* section click on the *Enable* button.

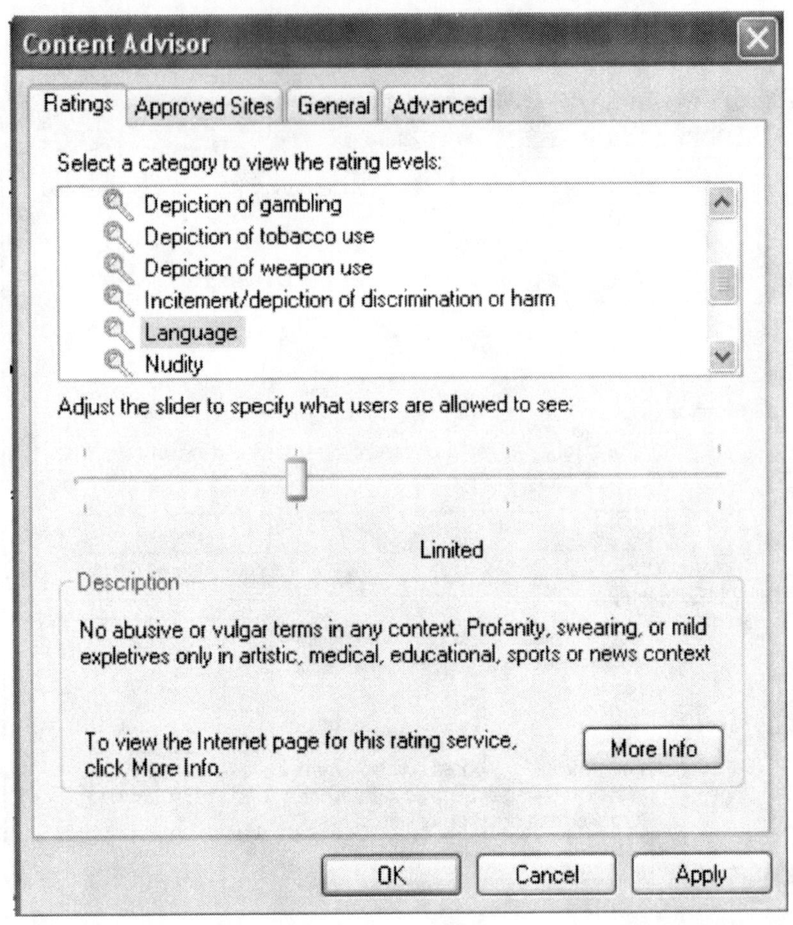

You will see the different types of filters the *Content Advisor* can use, and the slider will allow you to set the level of the filter. In this example, I selected the *Language* filter and set the slider to *Limited*. The slider has four settings under the *Language* filter: *None*, *Limited*, *Some* and *Unrestricted*. Not all filters have four settings. Select the setting that you feel is appropriate for your children. Note the *Description* of what content is being filtered. This setting will not allow “abusive or vulgar terms in any context” nor “profanity, swearing or mild expletives.” As you move the slider, you will see the description of what content is being filtered.

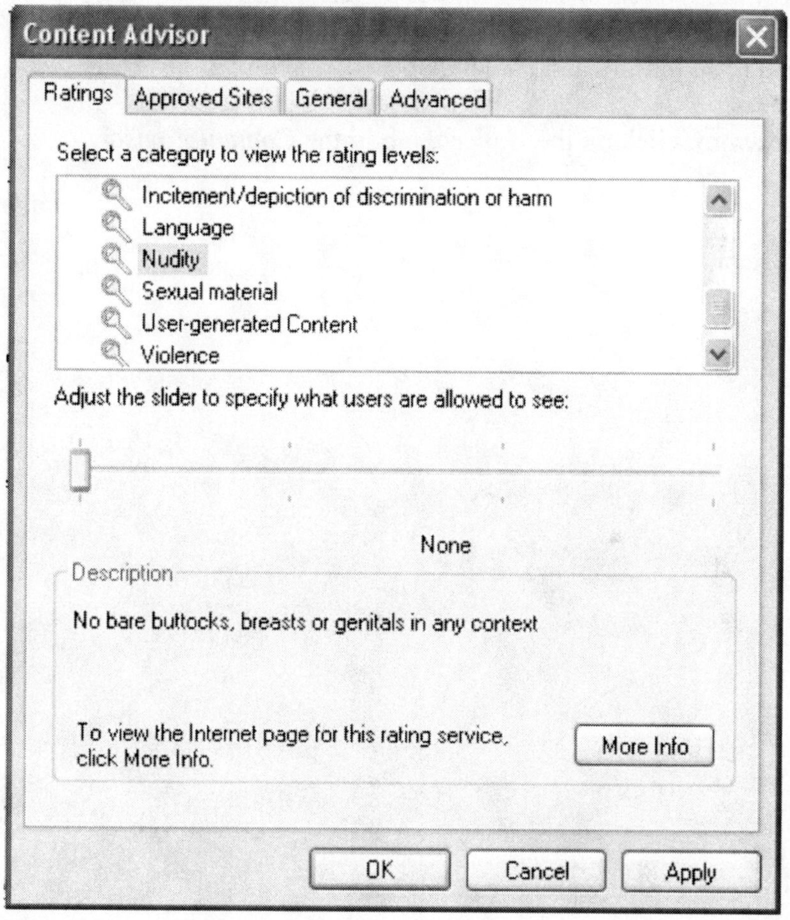

In this example, I used the *Nudity* filter and set the slider to *None*. In the description you can see this means no websites showing "bare buttocks, breasts or genitals in any context" will be allowed.

Now that you have set the slider, do not forget to use the *Password* feature so junior cannot change the filter settings. To set the password, click on the *General* tab in the *Content Advisor*.

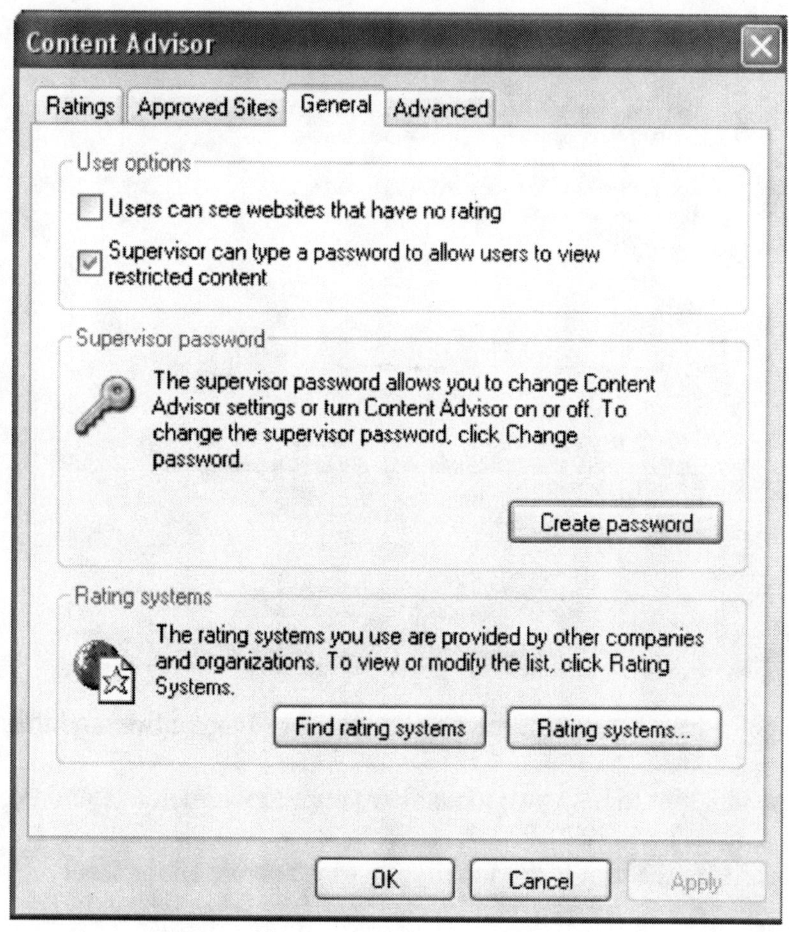

Click the *Create Password* button.

Type in your password, retype your password to confirm and then type in a hint to help you remember your password at a later date. Make sure the hint is not too cryptic as it may be a long time before you use this feature again.

Will setting these filters prevent a child from ever seeing any of the type of content being filtered? The answer is, "No." Not all web pages list ratings or have been rated. Because of this, some forbidden content may get through the filters, but having the filters working is much better than not. At times I hear the argument that no filter is 100 percent effective so why use them? Well, no seatbelt or airbag will guarantee 100 percent survival in an accident, but I am not about to start letting my child ride in or drive a car that does not have these features. Remember that as parents we are trying to do the best that we can for our children. I do not know any parents who can protect their children 100 percent of the time from getting a cold, a skinned knee or their feelings hurt at school, but that does not stop us from doing what we can to prevent these things as much as possible.

IV. Using Mozilla Firefox to Filter Content

The other browser I use is Mozilla Firefox. It allows you to select some of the same settings.

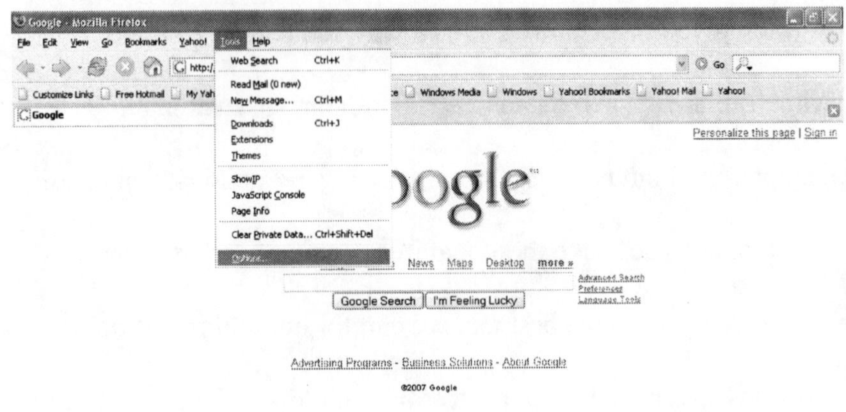

Before we look at *Tools* and *Options*, notice the *McAfee SiteAdvisor* button at the lower right corner of the screen. In Firefox it appears in the lower right corner and on IE 7 it appears in the upper left just below the URL. (URL stands for Uniform Resource Locator and has become the generic term for expressing a location on the internet. Think of the URL as the street address of the store you want to shop at or a friend you would like to visit. It would be difficult to remember the street address for every store you shop at or everyone you know. Yet from memory you know how to drive to each store or friend's home. The internet works in a similar fashion. Type in the name of the business you want to visit, add the extension for the type of site and the computers on the internet will "resolve" or change the alpha characters to numbers and take you to the location you are asking to visit.)

(Remember **Personal Favorite: McAfee SiteAdvisor**.) This feature is one more reason I like this program for my home computer because it gives me a review of the site I want to visit. It will warn me if there are links to unwanted content or unwanted programs that may run from the selected site. It will also tell me if I have visited the site before and if it is safe. The SiteAdvisor will change color depending on what type of site you are trying to visit. If you want to know more information about the site, you can hover over the *SiteAdvisor* button and a balloon will open with additional details about the site.

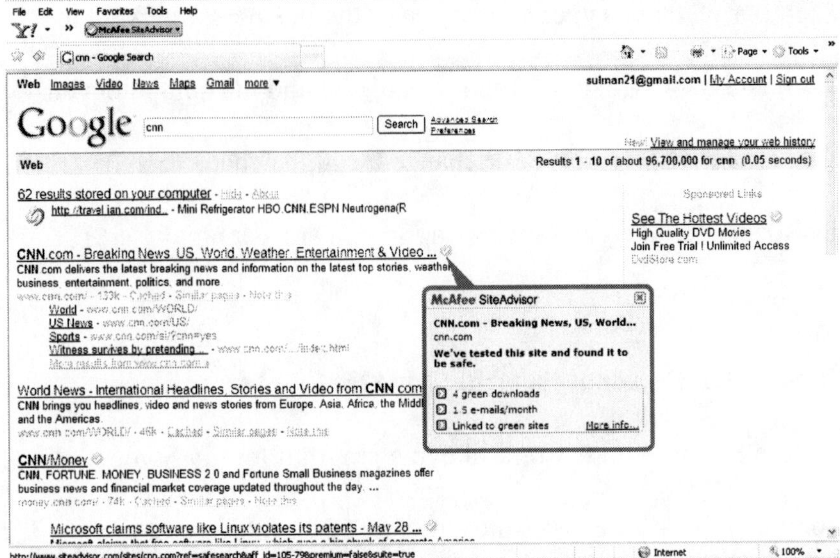

In this example you can see the site you are thinking of visiting received a safe rating. The site and links from the site received a "green" or safe recommendation.

Now, getting back to Firefox, next click on *Tools* and *Options*.

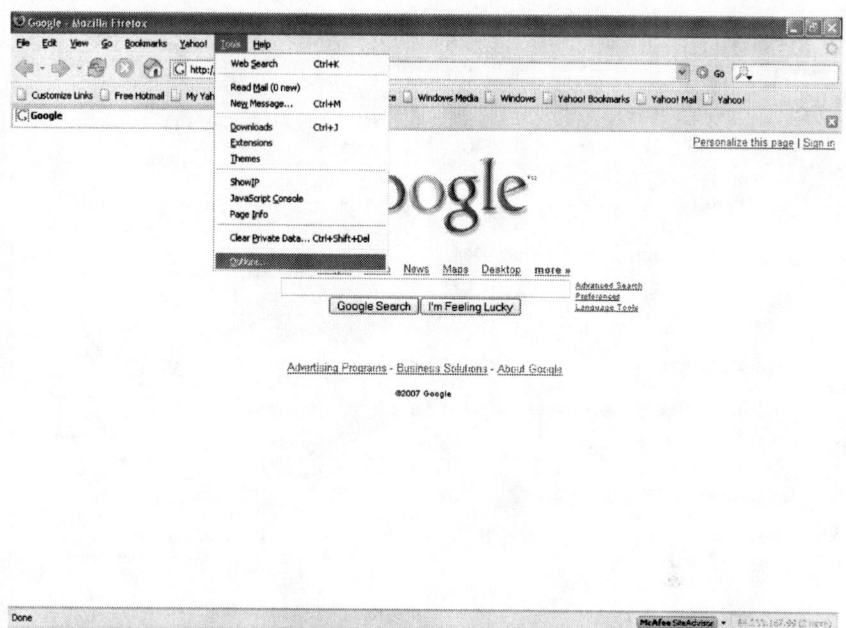

The *Options* window will open.

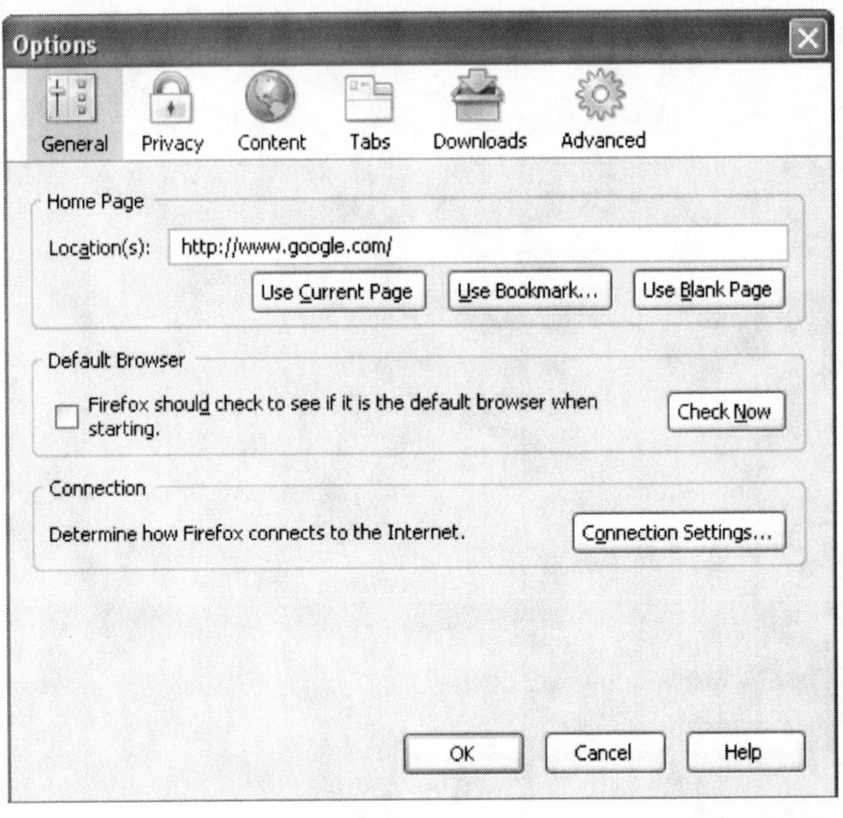

This is where you can set the home page for Firefox. Changing the home page for Firefox is the same as IE 7. Notice the home page is set as www.google.com. If Firefox were currently on a website other than Google, clicking the *Use Current Page* button would set whatever website is currently displayed by Firefox as the home page.

Next, click on the *Privacy* tab on top and the *History* tab in the middle of the screen to view how long the history is being saved.

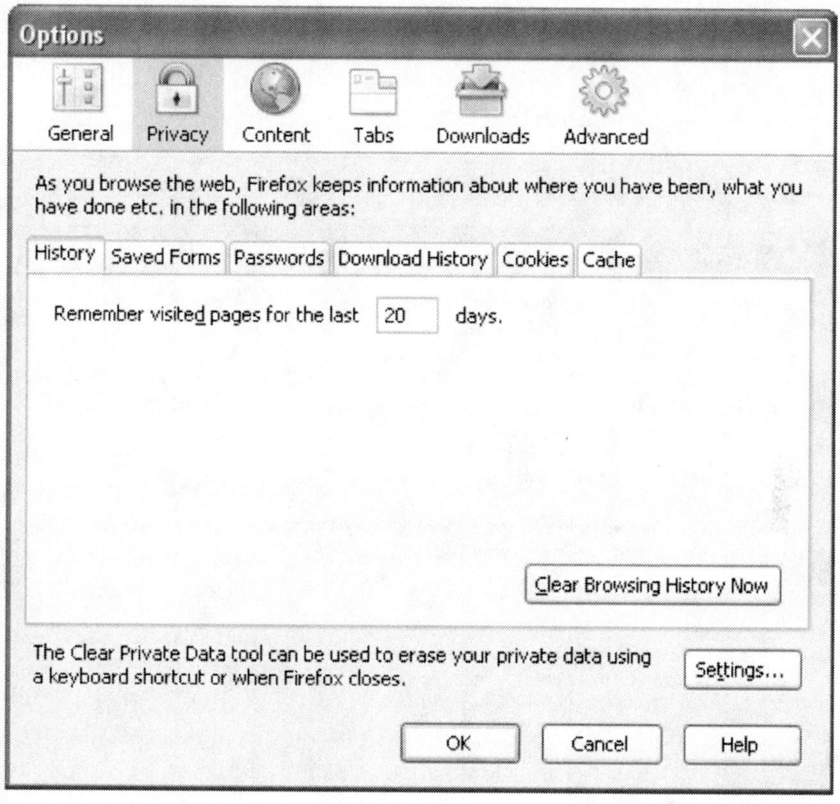

The default is also 20 days for Firefox. See if the default has been changed. Reset the number to what you feel is appropriate for your family.

Firefox will allow you to create a **master password** to protect all the other passwords you use to access websites. In other words, if you visit sites that require a password before the site is viewed, you can type it into Firefox and when the browser attempts to view the page, it will automatically transmit the password and enter the site.

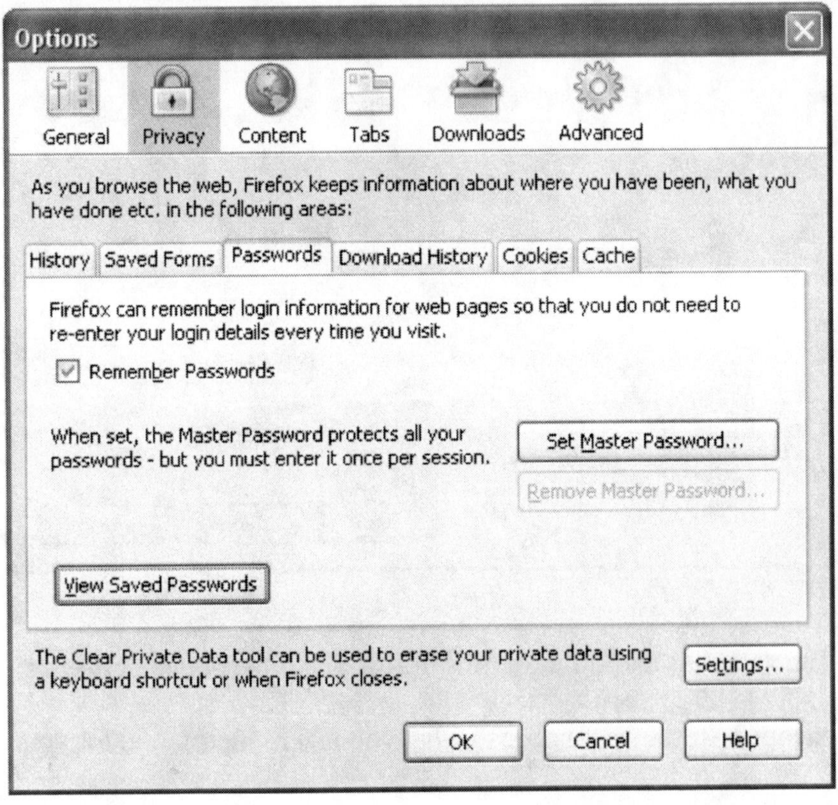

Click on the *Passwords* tab. From this window, you can view any passwords saved for specific web pages. You can edit those passwords so they can be changed or updated. Then click on *Set Master Password* to create a password that prevents anyone from entering this area and learning or changing your passwords. You will be required to type in the master password at the beginning of a session or when you first launch the browser. This means junior needs to know your master password to enter any of the sites that require a password. The advantage here is that you can enter the sites you frequently visit without having to remember each and every password because you only need to remember your master password. It also means junior would have to know your master password to visit those same sites.

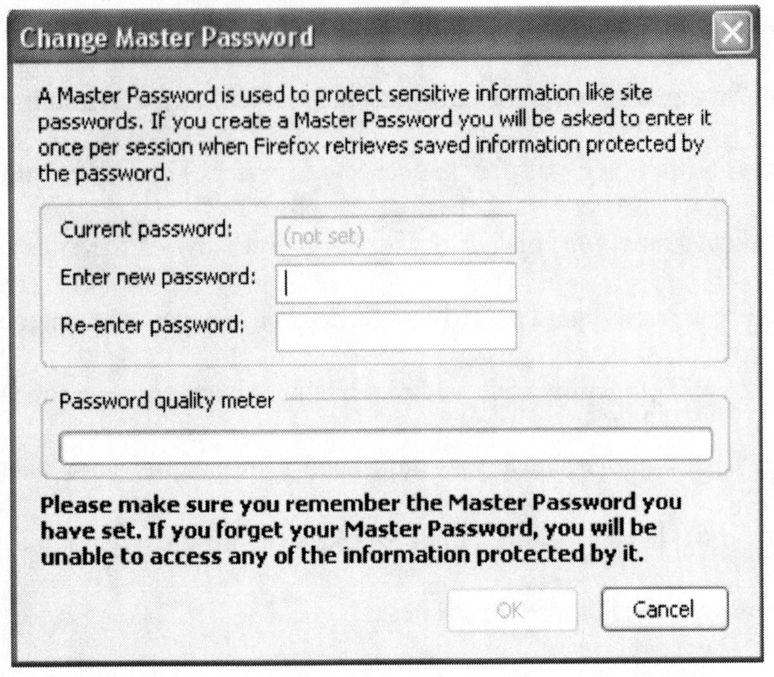

Type in your master password, then re-enter the password to confirm you typed it correctly. The password quality meter lets you know just how secure a password you have chosen. Remember, strong passwords are not simply a word or name. They contain a combination of letters, numbers and characters interspersed throughout the password. For example, the password "MICHAEL" would not be a very strong password. However, "M2I%C8H9A$E^L" would be a fairly strong password. The downside to this password is it is difficult to remember.

As for content filtering, you can select what sites you want to filter by selecting the *Content* tab.

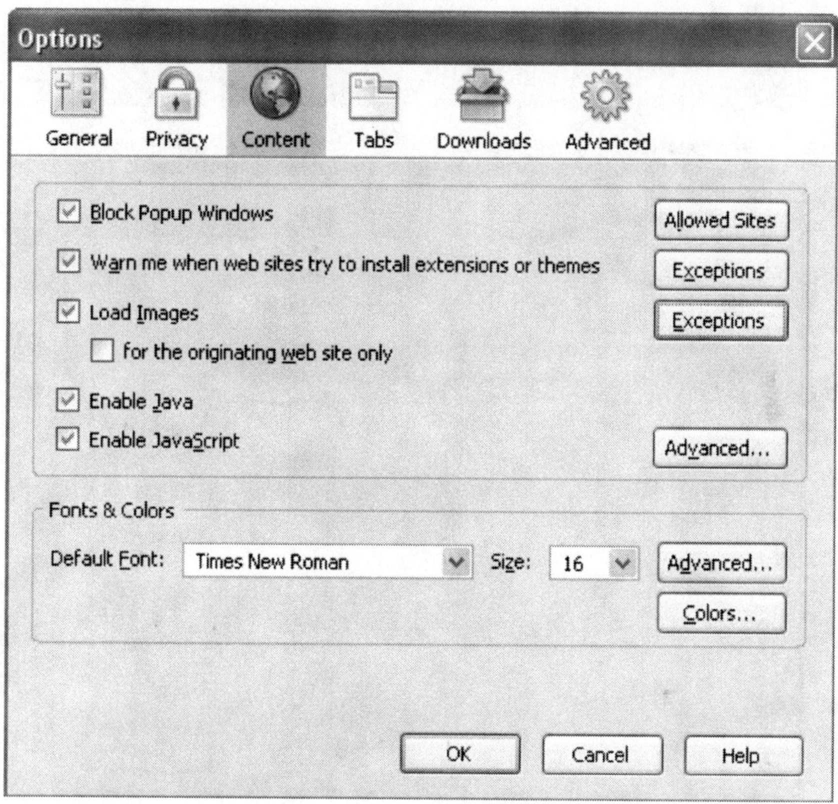

Click on either *Allowed Sites* or *Exceptions* to enter the address of sites you want to allow. These filters set what sites may open a popup window or allow extra content when you visit the site. Setting the *Exceptions* for websites that install extensions or themes allows those sites to add secondary programs that work in concert with the browser. The *Exceptions* for images allow you to select which websites can display images on your computer.

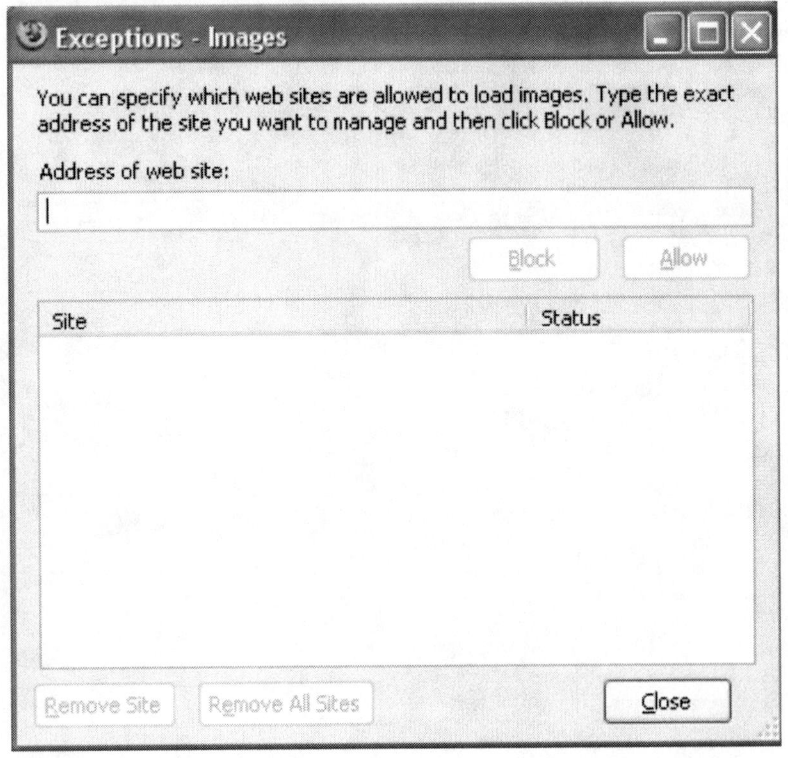

The problem with this type of filtering is you have to know the address for every site you will allow your child to visit.

V. Cyber Sentinel Parental Control

I prefer a different type of filtering software to protect my children. Using the settings in IE 7 and Firefox is a good start, but they do not have all the features I want. They also do not allow me to specifically tailor the filters to my family's needs. They do not allow me to block the information that would let an online predator to have face-to-face contact with my child. I will provide a full list of the information you should teach your child to protect in the "Library Settings" section of this chapter.

I would also like the parental control program to send me notification when a mistake has been made. I want to know what personal information my child is sending and to whom that information was sent. I want this done in a simple, user-friendly interface that will not frustrate a parent and does not cost a fortune. Most good programs cost about $40.00, which is less than you would spend on one video game. My **Personal Favorite** is **Cyber Sentinel**.

Cyber Sentinel®

There are many reasons I prefer Cyber Sentinel. I find the interface to be easy to use and easy for novice parents to navigate. This one program will work with almost all the programs online predators will use to groom your children. This program will monitor web browsing, instant messages, email, peer-to-peer programs and, if your child tries to use a word processing program to type messages and attach them to an email, the program will detect violations in a word processing program.

You can purchase the program as an install for your home computer only, or you can purchase the web version which allows you to install the program on your home computer but control and review the program remotely by signing on to a website. This means that if you need to review what is occurring at home, or if you need to change a setting to allow a specific topic to be researched for homework, you can change the settings via the web from work, while traveling or any place you can access the internet. This product also has a built-in predator library which allows the program to review chats, instant messages, emails or other types of communications for language that is predatory in nature. The program not only looks for conversations of a sexual nature, although those conversations would be captured, but also for statements of a grooming nature. It then warns the parents of these statements.

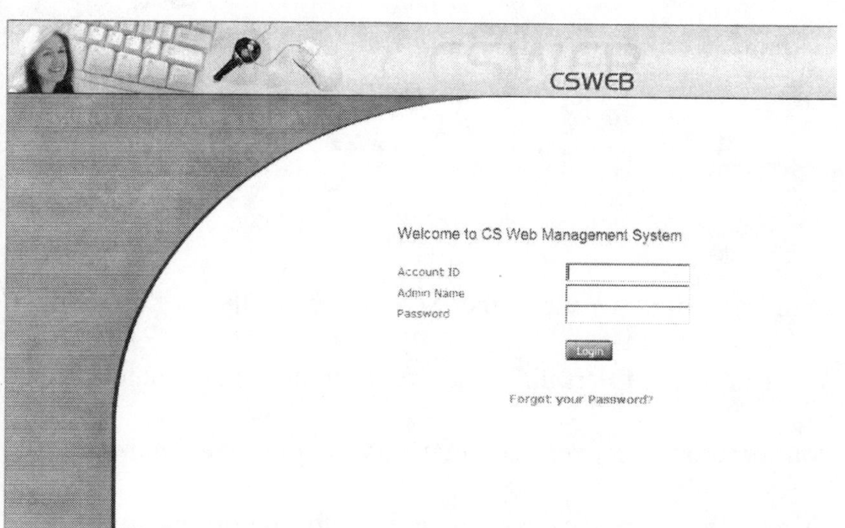

Above is the web version's log-on screen. As you can see, the account allows the Administrator to log-in and control the program.

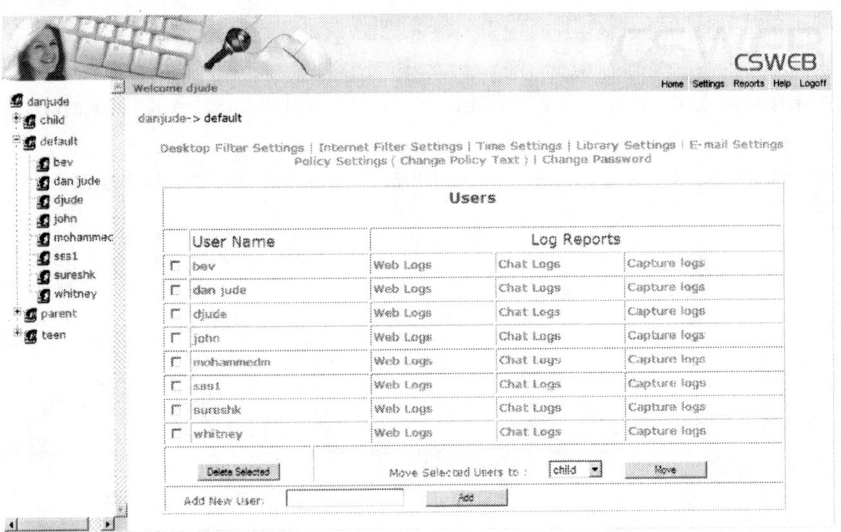

In the left window pane, Cyber Sentinel shows the user accounts. You can set the filters differently for each user. For example, if you want to restrict your children's ability to visit e-commerce sites (online shopping), you do not have to shut off the program every time you want to shop online. The settings for your account would still allow you to do that type of activity, even though the settings for your children's accounts would restrict it when they are online. One of the key features of this program is the ability to tailor it specifically for your family.

Across the top of the large window you can see the different types of filters: *Desktop*, *Internet*, *Times*, *Library*, *E-mail* and *Policy Settings*. The Policy Settings can be used as a warning to children each time they sign-on. At the Illinois Attorney General's Office we created an online contract that parents and children can review, sign and post next to the computer. That way, if the child has any doubts about what conduct is allowed they can check the agreement (you can find the agreement at http://www.illinoisattorneygeneral.gov/children/internet_agreement.pdf). With Cyber Sentinel you can create a Policy Statement for you home.

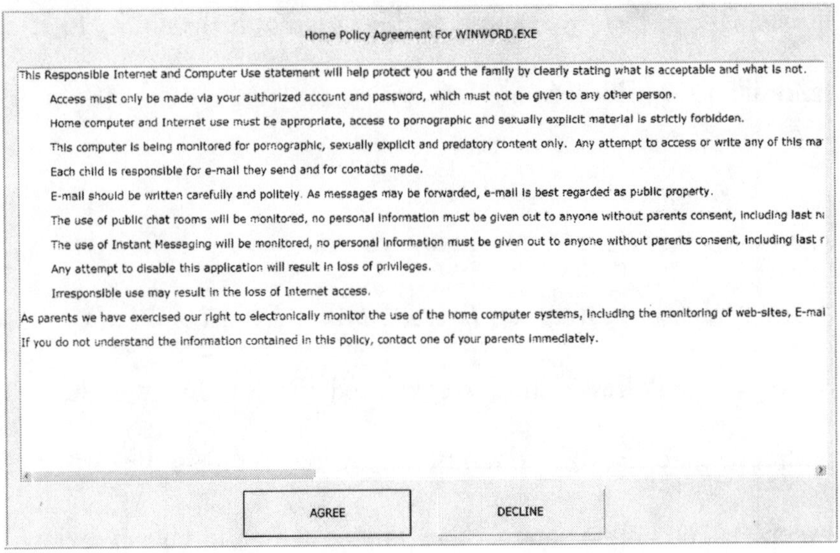

Home Policy Agreement For WINWORD.EXE

This Responsible Internet and Computer Use statement will help protect you and the family by clearly stating what is acceptable and what is not.

Access must only be made via your authorized account and password, which must not be given to any other person.

Home computer and Internet use must be appropriate, access to pornographic and sexually explicit material is strictly forbidden.

This computer is being monitored for pornographic, sexually explicit and predatory content only. Any attempt to access or write any of this ma

Each child is responsible for e-mail they send and for contacts made.

E-mail should be written carefully and politely. As messages may be forwarded, e-mail is best regarded as public property.

The use of public chat rooms will be monitored, no personal information must be given out to anyone without parents consent, including last n

The use of Instant Messaging will be monitored, no personal information must be given out to anyone without parents consent, including last r

Any attempt to disable this application will result in loss of privileges.

Irresponsible use may result in the loss of Internet access.

As parents we have exercised our right to electronically monitor the use of the home computer systems, including the monitoring of web-sites, E-mai

If you do not understand the information contained in this policy, contact one of your parents immediately.

AGREE DECLINE

I recommend setting the Initial Policy to run at every log-in. This way, every time your child signs on they see a reinforcement of the online agreement.

One of the most common questions parents ask is, “Should I tell my child that I am monitoring activity on the computer?” My answer is, “Yes.” Let your children know that you are monitoring what they do on the home computer. You should let them know what is acceptable and what is unacceptable. The online agreement can serve as a guide. Alter it to fit your family’s needs. That agreement can then be entered into the Policy Statement. Your child will see the statement each time the computer is turned on, reinforcing what is allowed and what is prohibited. Know this: your children will make mistakes. Do not become overly upset. Work with your children to help them understand why what they did was wrong and how to avoid it in the future. If your child fears being yelled at or punished for telling you about something they did online, they will be less willing to communicate and they will likely try to hide things from you. They will begin to believe that keeping things secret is better and that the online predators are telling them the truth. Because the online predator's strongest weapon is secrecy, your strongest defense is having a relationship with your children in which they are not afraid to communicate with you.

Setting the filters is simple. Simply select the user name from the left window pane and set the program *Mode*, *Violation Detection*, *Policy View* and *Library* options.

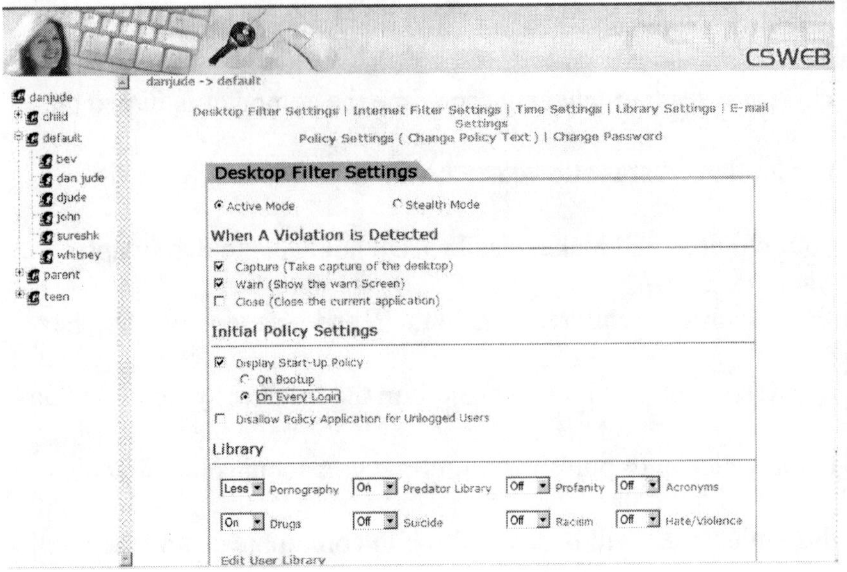

The difference between *Active* and *Stealth Mode* is notification on screen that the program is running. If you have told your child you are monitoring computer use, then click on *Active Mode*. If you have decided not to tell your children, click on *Stealth Mode* so the program will run in the background without your child's knowledge.

If a violation occurs you have several *Violation Detection Settings*. The program can simply capture a screen shot (geek for picture) of the desktop at the time of the violation. This will provide a picture of what was occurring on the computer at the time of the violation. In the case of an instant message from a predator, the picture would show the date, time, instant messaging client in use, the user name for the online predator, the content that caused the violation and possibly a full page of instant messages between your child and the online predator. You can then discuss the violation with your child and, if you are satisfied with your child's answers, let the issue end. If you were concerned that the online predator's intentions were to harm your child, you can print out the capture with all the above information and give it to your local police department. Armed with the screen name, instant messaging client, date and time, they may be able to identify the online predator. Yes, just having this basic information can lead to the identification of an online predator.

The next option is to have the program take a capture of the offending content and then issue a warning to the user. This warning is done in the *Active Mode*. Once a capture of the offending content is taken, a screen will be displayed informing the user of the violation.

After the warning, the prohibited screen will disappear and the user can return to the activity they were engaged in before the notification of the violation.

If you want to take it a step further, click on all three *Violation Settings*: *Capture*, *Warn* and *Close*. With these settings chosen, the program will conduct a capture of the violating content, issue a warning screen announcing the activity was prohibited and then close the offending program. If your child was surfing the web, the browser would be closed. If your child was instant messaging, the instant messaging client would be closed. Your child can re-open the program and start again; however, every time they are involved in some type of violating content the program will shut down the offending program.

It didn't take very long for my children's friends to realize that any use of profanity during an instant message with my children will cause them to be kicked out of the instant message. It only took a few sessions for his friends to clean up the language. Of course, I received emails on each of the violations. It got to the point that my son would call me at work before the email arrived to let me know what was going on. I have to admit, I enjoyed the interruptions at work to have a conversation with my son.

Most importantly, the program reviews content from both sides of the conversations, so whether your child said something that caused a violation or the predator used prohibited language in their effort to groom your child, the program will shut down the violating chat, instant message or website.

Choosing a Library to use will depend on the age, maturity level and computer expertise of your child. Younger children may need heavy filtering. Computer-literate children who are not very mature may also need heavy filtering. However, like any other privilege, as your children grow, mature and demonstrate discipline and good judgment, you can decrease the level of filtering. Keep in mind, you only have a short period of time to instill the moral values and proper conduct guidelines you want your child to learn. By the time they reach 18, they may be out the door, possibly on their way to college, entering the military or going off to live on their own. If you kept the filtering at an extremely high level, they will not have learned the discipline needed to cope on their own.

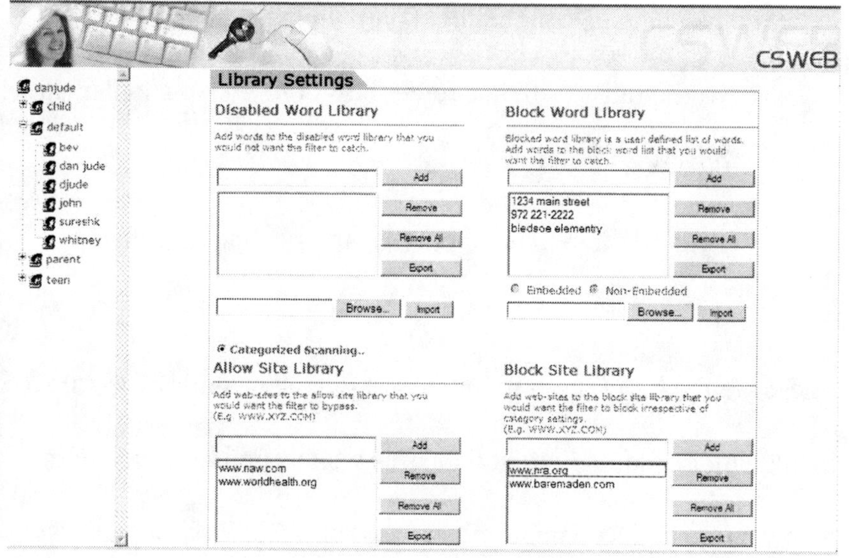

Probably the most important feature is the *Block Word Library*. This is where you enter the terms that you do not want your child sending out online. I recommend blocking:

- your first and last names
- your home telephone number
- your child's cell phone number
- your street address
- your home town/city of residence
- your zip code (this is pretty much the same as telling anyone the name of your home town)
- the name of your child's school

- the name of your child's favorite playground or park
- your child's birthdate (enter it as 00/00/00 and as January 00, 0000)
- your credit card numbers (so junior cannot use them online)

These are the basic items to enter; you may have others. Be sure to include mom and dad's first names as well as junior's. Predators who want to abduct a child might show up at their school and say, "I'm a friend of your mom and she asked me to pick you up from school today" to fool the child into going with them. If the predator knows the parents' first names it might be easier to convince the child that this is a friend of his or her parents.

Once these terms are entered, the program knows it cannot let them be sent on- or offline. What does that mean? It means that the program will monitor chats, instant messages, blogs, email and even word processing, and if it is alerted to the use of any of the prohibited content it will block the content from leaving your computer. It will then follow the *Violation Detection Settings* you have chosen: capture, warn, close and then send you a notification of the violation. It will notify you in real time if junior did something wrong on the computer. All you have to do is supply the program with your email address and it will send you a notice of the violation instantly.

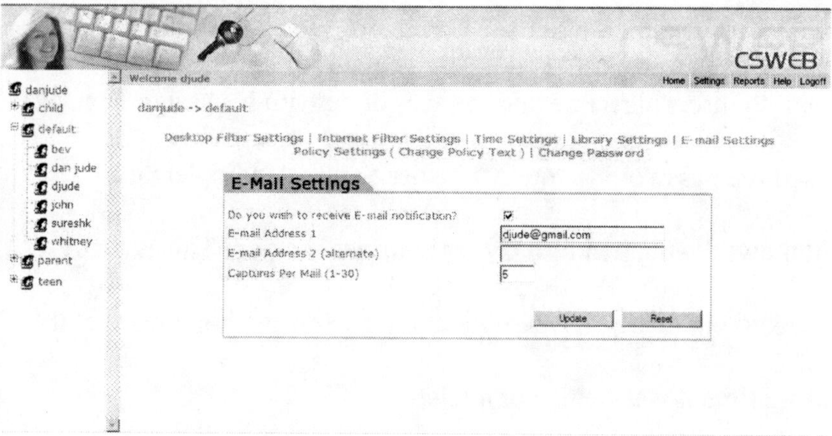

This is another feature I really like. I do not know many parents who have an extra hour or two each day or five to six hours each week to sit down and read through a log of all the violations that have occurred. With email notification you will know quickly what junior is up to at home.

Now please, learn from my mistakes here: I loaded the program, put in our last name and let it run. My son (by the way he is not a "junior") sat down to do his homework and the first thing he put on his paper was his name. The program snapped into action, captured the violating content, sent a warning and promptly closed the word processing program. I got the email at work at the moment my wife was listening to our son complain. We had to teach him to wait to insert his name until he was done with his assignment. We used the password to turn off Cyber Sentinel, complete the homework and then turn Cyber Sentinel back on. This actually worked out nicely, as my wife could review the homework at the same time it was being completed.

Cyber Sentinel has many other features that can help you control your children's access. The *Time Management* feature allows you to designate when different user accounts can be online.

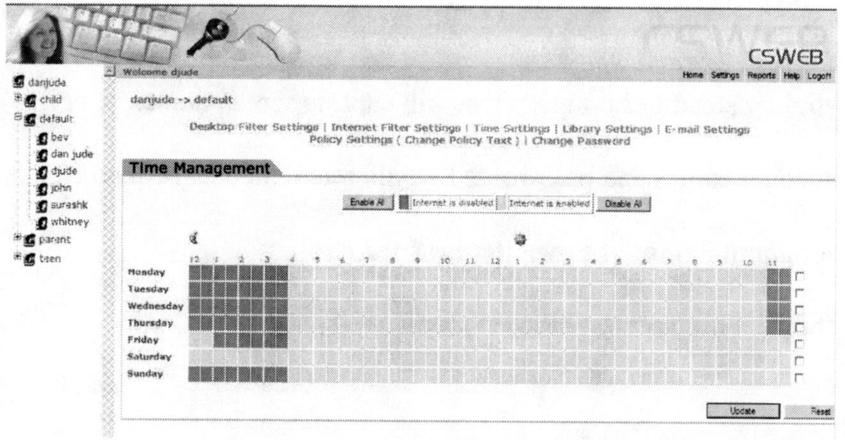

Select the user, then select the times the internet may be accessed. You can set the bulk of the time for after school but before bedtime. This would be prime homework time. In the old days, when I was growing up, I had to come inside when the street lights came on. My father said, "There is nothing you can do outside after the street lights come on except get in trouble." The Time Management feature is a digital version of my father's saying. There is no reason your child should be on the internet late at night. This feature can help you prevent them from sneaking online after everyone has gone to sleep.

VI. Spector Pro Key Logger

If you find you have a very computer-literate child and need a slightly stealthier program that will capture screen names, user account names and passwords I would recommend a different program. **Personal Favorite: Spector Pro** (http://www.spectorsoft.com/products).

At times, I hear from parents who are concerned that their children are hiding their online activity, and the parents are not computer literate enough to find the content. This usually involves online journals, blogs or social networking sites. (I will deal with these in more details in the next chapter.) Parents ask, “How do I see the content my child has online?” The answer is to view the site created by your child. That is usually followed by, "I tried but it is marked private and I cannot see it."

At this time, you have to decide if you are going to confront your child and demand to see the content and know the password. However, be aware that children have been known to create multiple accounts online. They let their parents see the "clean" site and never reveal the other online accounts.

Spector Pro is a key logging software that even your computer-literate child will not know is running because it runs in the background on your home computer. You need to know a specific set of keystrokes to find the program on your computer because it installs and runs in a stealth mode. Without the knowledge of the keys and password, your children will not find the program or be able to delete information captured by the program. Since it is a "key logger" is will literally record every keystroke typed on your keyboard. The program will record many areas of computer activity:

- instant messages
- chat messages
- social networking sites and passwords
- online account creation including user name and password
- email activity including email address and password
- search terms (Is your child seeking dangerous material?)
- websites visited
- programs used
- daily activity
- keyword search

Spector Pro uses a simple interface to allow you to see the history and content of activity on your computer. Think of it as a stenographer and closed circuit camera for your home computer. It will record all the websites visited and take screen captures of the content of the websites. It will record all incoming and outgoing emails with complete content. This means you will know to whom and from whom your child is sending and receiving emails, what they are discussing in the emails and if they are headed down a dangerous path.

One of the questions parents ask is, "How can I tell who my child is talking to online and what are they saying?" This program will record instant message sessions for America Online/AIM, MSN Messenger, Yahoo! Messenger and many other instant message clients. Some of the instant messaging and chat clients do have built-in logs. However, those logs must be turned on and can easily be deleted by any user on the computer. This program will capture the online conversations line by line and allow you, as the parent, to evaluate the content of the conversation. In extreme cases it could provide invaluable information as to whom your child was chatting with and where your child is heading, should they decide to meet with an online predator.

Since the program captures all keystrokes, it can provide the usernames for email or online accounts and it can supply the sign-on or screen names for chat and or instant messaging clients. Most importantly, it will also display the password for each of these activities. Now instead of depending on your child to show you the website (and perhaps only seeing the "clean version"), you will have a list of all the online accounts. You can review each site, including both the "clean" and the "dangerous" sites, and then talk to your child. Armed with all the information, you can formulate a strategy to educate your child about suspect sites, content and users.

The fact is, as parents, we look at those people who have conversations and contact with our children very differently than our children do. I know teachers understand this better than most parents. The language and behavior they see in schools would send most of us over the edge. Yet teachers understand that this language and content is part of fitting in, maturing and learning how to exist at school. We see the world through the eyes of our past experiences, experiences our children have not had, do not understand and cannot use as a point of reference for their online contact.

At times, the conversations our children have may alarm us. However, that same conversation with an explanation from our children may turn out to be harmless. You will not know this until you have spoken to your child. When you speak to your child, do so with an open mind. Be prepared to learn that the conversation you read was not the conversation your child had (due to the social and cultural differences between you and your child). We have all received an email message that upset us at first, and then we later learned the true meaning of the email once we learned the context. Conversations typed in emails, chats and instant messaging do not convey emotional states very well. It is easy to misread the emotion in an online communication and interpret a message incorrectly.

Remember, the reason for the conversation is not to punish, but to *learn*. That learning is for both children *and* parents.

Now that we understand how our computer works and have the programs installed that will give us some peace of mind, let's move on to the next chapter and talk about the online predators.

CHAPTER 3: ONLINE PREDATORS

I. Who Are They?

I wish I could tell you exactly what an online predator looks like so that you could check all the images sent to your child and know if they are chatting to an online predator. Unfortunately, it is not as simple as: "Online predator = creepy-looking individual who is balding, short, fat with scraggly facial hair, bad teeth, a limited education and frequents virtual playgrounds and malls."

In the nearly 15 years I have worked in computer crimes and child exploitation I have learned that there is no particular "look" that all online predators share. I know some of my colleagues will say after an arrest, "He just looks like a child predator." Well, now that he is wearing a jail-issued jumpsuit, he does indeed look like a child predator. However, when he drove up in his car, got out and walked up to the meeting location, he looked like every other person in the world.

The online predators we have arrested come from every walk of life. We have arrested ministers, doctors, lawyers, soldiers, police officers, teachers, information technology specialists and day care workers. They have ranged in age from 18 to 75 years old (yes, 75 years of age). In fact, one person we arrested a few years back still holds the record for exaggerating his age online. When the solicitation began, the predator claimed that he was 27. Three months later when he was arrested, he turned out to be in his 60s!

I can give you some broad observations about the people that I have arrested or who have been arrested by some of the agencies who are members of the Child Exploitation Task Force. From those observations I would say *an online predator is most likely to be a white male who is 18 to 65 years of age*.

I know this is not much information, but the fact is, most of the people arrested for these types of crimes are white males. At times, females are arrested for sexual exploitation of children. However, they make up a small portion of the total arrests. The predators we arrested came from varied backgrounds. Some were employed in white collar jobs, including CEOs and educators with doctorate degrees, some worked blue collar jobs that gave them access to children and still others were unemployed. Some had college educations and advanced degrees. while some of the people arrested have not even received a high school diploma. For some, this may be the first time they have been arrested. Take note, I said first time *arrested*, and not the first time they have committed a criminal act of child exploitation. This just happens to be the first time they were *caught*. One study revealed that a "typical" offender may commit as many as 117 acts of molestation. Many have repeat offenses for sexual crimes against children. Some are single with no children; others are married with many children. Most of the time, online predators have children who are far older then the children they are soliciting or seeking to victimize.

The simple fact is, online predators come in all shapes, sizes and backgrounds. Because of this, there is no easy way to know if your child is chatting to an online predator.

For a more in-depth look at the makeup of online predators arrested by law enforcement, you can read the *Internet Sex Crimes Against Minors: The Response of Law Enforcement* report by the National Center for Missing and Exploited Children, the Office of Juvenile Justice and Delinquency Prevention and the Crimes Against Children Research Center. It can be found on the web page for the National Center for Missing and Exploited Children at http://www.missingkids.com/missingkids/servlet/ResourceServlet?LanguageCountry=en_US&PageId=1456.

II. Online Predator "Grooming"

There are certain types of questions online predators ask. Knowing the reasoning behind these questions can help you to educate your children. Being aware of these "grooming" questions can prepare your child to identify dangerous contacts and alert you to that contact if it happens.

We typically teach our children that when someone in a car pulls up and asks them for directions, they should *not* approach the car.

In fact, they should run away from the car and tell their parents. We teach them that the person in the car might not really have been asking for directions. What they were really saying is, "Are you foolish enough to come close to my car so I can pull you inside?" When a predator holding a dog leash approaches and asks for assistance in finding his lost dog, we tell our children not to go with that person because there probably is no dog, and the predator was really asking, "Are you foolish enough to leave a place of safety and walk away with a stranger?" In the same fashion, we need to teach our children what might really be behind the questions online predators ask.

Not all predators will act the same way online. Some will be very cautious and take time to groom your child. They need to be sure your child and your computer will not alert you to their presence. They may test your child through a series of requests, with the theme being that this is a "secret relationship," and "we both would be in trouble if your parents find out." Other online predators will be direct and ask your child to leave home immediately.

In one case, we had an undercover account of a boy, approximately 12 years old, online at about ten o'clock at night. We observed the arrival of an instant message. The instant message asked, "Do you want to f—k?" (The original message actually spelled the entire word.) At first we thought the instant message was from another police officer who had attended some training we taught. We thought the police officer remembered the screen name of our "child" and was playing a prank on the teacher. We responded, "Do I know you?" We realized that did not sound like a real 12-year-old boy. A real 12-year-old boy probably would have ignored the instant message altogether. In response to our question we got:

"No, I am a 40-something businessman who flies around the country. When I land, I get online and look for all the young dudes. I see if they want to hookup for sex. I am at such and such hotel, room number 12345. Do you want to come over and have sex?"

By this time it was after normal shift hours and that meant overtime for the entire team. Being prudent (well, at a certain supervisor's direction), we did not spend the overtime. We let the online predator know that our mother was home and we could not sneak out right then. We asked if we could come by tomorrow after school (when it would be a regular scheduled shift and not incur an overtime expense). The online predator said, "Yes, that would be fine and, oh, by the way, when you come here this is what I want to do with you…." The online predator sent 12 images of children engaging in sexual conduct with adults. The images included children as young as toddlers. Yes, two- or three-year-old children! The online predator asked if that was acceptable. Since the solicitation to have sex with a minor is a felony and each one of the images was an additional felony charge, we let him know that as far as we (the police officers) were concerned, 13 chargeable felonies was indeed "fine" with us.

The next day, we went to the hotel and arrested the predator. We found he was telling the truth about traveling around the country.

We attempted to find every child he molested in each state and have him charged in every state in which he had committed a crime.

I wish I could say this is abnormal for contact between an online predator and a child but it is not. Many online predators will be this direct with your children. They will request a meeting with your child almost immediately. Others may take longer, but once they are satisfied they are chatting to a child, they will request a meeting. The meeting is specifically for the purpose of having sexual contact with the child.

What questions should I tell my children to be aware of as predatory?

1. ***Where is your computer?***

   a. This question is designed to act as a threat assessment for the online predator. The online predator is checking the likelihood of being caught by chatting or instant messaging a child at this computer. Is the computer in a location that that allows everyone in the family to use the computer? Can mom and dad see what is being said on the monitor? If your child told the online predator the computer was located in the kitchen, family room or great room, the online contact would probably be terminated by the online predator. If your child responded that the computer is in their room, the conversation would probably continue.

b. If the online predator does continue the conversation, the topic will probably become sexual within the next few questions.

2. ***Who uses your computer?***

a. This is another question designed to act as a threat assessment for the online predator. If your child were to reply, "The computer is mine," the predator will probably continue with the conversation. The fact that parents or any other family members do not use the computer would make the online predator feel safer about speaking in a sexual manner to the child and not fear being caught. However, if your child responded, "Everyone in the family uses the computer," the online predator would probably terminate the contact.

Question behind the questions: "Will anyone other than the child using this computer see or know that I am soliciting a child for sex?"

Online predators will often ask questions number one and two at the same time. *Any answers to the first two questions that indicate other family members (especially parents) use the computer will probably terminate the contact. There are enough unprotected children online that an online predator does not need to risk talking to this child. He will move on to find an unprotected child. We learn from this that* **the best place to put your computer is in a public area and the worst place is in your child's bedroom.**

3. Do you have any brothers or sisters?

a. This is another type of threat assessment question. Is there a brother or sister in the family who may learn about our online relationship? Will you speak to your brother or sister and tell them about the online predator's requests?

b. Will your brother or sister tell mom and dad if they learn about the relationship either by talking to you or by finding out about our contact via evidence on the family computer?

Question behind the question: "How safe is it to start to groom this child?"

4. What is your address or phone number?

a. Providing this type of information can allow an online predator to conduct a surveillance of your child as they come and go from school.

b. Most people do not realize that their phone number is tied to their address which makes it easy for an online predator to find out where you and your child live.

Question behind the question: "Can I use the information to actually find you in real life, whether you want me to find you or not?"

5. ***Are you active?***

   a. This question means, "Are you having sex?" "Active" means having sexual contact with someone, and this question would likely be followed up with, "What have you done?" The online predator will ask very specific questions concerning masturbation, oral sex and sexual intercourse. Most of the questions are blunt. Most parents would be very alarmed at this type of content being discussed with their children in this manner.

   b. This question may be phrased as, "*Are you a virgin?*" The online predator will tell younger children with no sexual history that it will be a better experience to have their first sexual encounter with an older person. He will explain that children their own age will not care for them in the way that an older person will because they do not have the same compassion or patience.

Question behind the question: "Are you sexually inexperienced, so when I tell you what is 'normal' you will accept it as fact? Will you accept that degradation or lying is part of a loving relationship?"

6. Do you masturbate?

a. Online predators will ask your child if he or she masturbates. They will tell your child that they masturbate. Some will tell your child that they masturbate four, five or six times a day. They will explain that everyone masturbates and that it is normal. Their goal is to convince your child to masturbate. The predator will ask your child to explain what they are doing as they masturbate. When the predator thinks your child has been groomed properly, he will ask your child to document their sexual conduct with digital photography.

b. *This type of questioning coupled with digital photography or streaming video can be very dangerous to your child.* The predator will use his webcam to send streaming video of himself masturbating. The online predator will repeat this behavior as many times as necessary to convince your child that masturbating and sending streaming video of the activity is "normal." Once the predator is sure your child is ready, he will ask the child to turn on his or her webcam, disrobe and masturbate. If your child does not have a webcam or digital camera, the online predator may offer to buy and mail a webcam or digital camera to your child. Be aware of what items are coming through the front door of your home. When we ask children why they agreed to the requests of the online predator, they told us, "He was my friend, my only real friend outside my family. He kept asking me to do it over and over and over. He would ask every time I was online, so I thought I would do it one time and he would be satisfied. I thought if I did it just that one time, he would still like me and be my friend and stop asking me. However, after I did it he still wanted me to masturbate and do more things on webcam." ("More things" usually involve inserting foreign objects into different body orifices.) When the child responded that they did not want to masturbate on camera any more, they were faced with the predator threatening them. They are told that the online predator recorded the streaming video or kept the digital images he had promised to delete and that unless your child agrees to continue the behavior, the video or images would be emailed to everyone at their junior high school. This is when it is difficult for parents not to overreact. Remember, if your child is afraid of being punished, they will not come to you for help. Let them know that no matter what they did, they can come to you for help in fixing the problem. I realize that in this situation you will need the patience of a Saint not to overreact. You must fight the urge to be angry at your child and realize that what they need from you is support, not punishment.

c. In this case you would need to contact a computer-literate police officer for assistance. Start with your local police department or sheriff's office. If they do not have someone trained to do the investigation you can get assistance from two locations. First, try www.icactraining.org. This site lists the commander of each of the Internet Crimes Against Children Task Forces in the United States. You will find the contact name, telephone number and email address. The second location is www.ncmec.org. Click on *CyberTipline* to go to a page where you can report any crime of child exploitation. The report can be made anonymously if you wish. The website belongs to the National Center for Missing and Exploited Children. They will accept the report, do a background investigation and route the case to a computer-literate police officer in the jurisdiction where the online predator lives. They can send the case anywhere in the world. You can find more information about the Internet Crimes Against Children Task Force and the National Center for Missing and Exploited Children in the Resource section of this book.

d. Keep digital photography and webcams away from children. They do not have the maturity to understand the dangers of using these devices. Online images are not like images printed on paper. You do not have to give away your copy of a digital image in order to trade with someone. You can send someone a copy of your computer file and still retain the original file on your computer. In time, the number of copies grows exponentially and it becomes impossible to know how many copies there are in existence. That is why it is almost impossible to remove an image from the internet once it has been sent to an online predator or posted to a website, blog or social networking site. We will look at this problem in more detail in the next chapter on social networking.

Question behind the question: "Can I get this child to masturbate on camera so I can get and possibly trade the video or images on the internet?" or "Can I get images to use to blackmail the child into continuing the contact and sexual activity?"

7. ***Do you have a digital camera or web camera?***

   a. As we discussed earlier, online predators will ask your children to use a digital camera to take pictures when they are nude or masturbating. If your child does not have a digital camera or web camera the online predator may offer to buy one for them. If your child gave the predator your home address, the camera can be sent in the mail, or worse, the online predator could drive to your home and leave it hidden outside the residence. They will tell your child during an instant message where to find the camera. The requests will continue until your child gives in, and then the online predator will use the images or streaming video to blackmail your child into providing additional images and video.

b. Do not forget a digital camera may be hidden in that new cell phone you just bought your child. Just because the resolution on the cell phone camera is not as good as a regular digital camera does not mean it is any safer.

Question behind the question: "Will I need to supply you with the technology so I can get the images or streaming video that will allow me to control your actions?"

8. Can you keep this a secret?

a. This question may be posed in many ways:

i. Will you tell anyone?

ii. You know if you tell anyone about me I will get in trouble; will you tell your mom or dad?

iii. If you tell your mom and dad about this you will get in trouble, but I will get in even more

trouble because I could go to jail. Do you want me to go to jail?

iv. Did you tell your best friend about us?

b. Again, these are threat assessment questions to gauge how safe it is to be chatting with your child. These are also grooming questions. They are used to establish a feeling of "trust" between the online predator and your child. First, the predator will try testing your child by asking him or her to keep minor and somewhat unimportant facts a secret. When your child proves he or she can keep a secret, the predator will compliment him or her for being a good friend. This type of grooming and complimenting will increase as the level of risk increases.

c. This question can also be asked about images that were sent:

i. Did you like my nude image?

ii. Do you still have my nude image?

iii. Did you tell anyone you saw my nude image?

In fact, the image sent may not even be an image of the online predator. It could be some pornographic image found online that the predator is passing off as a personal image. The predator may send streaming video but never show his face on camera. He may never show his face in a nude image or video. Or, he may show his face after he is comfortable it is safe to do so; in other words, when it seems like your child has been successfully groomed to not tell anyone about seeing the nude images or video.

Question behind the question: "Will this child report me to his or her parents when the conversation turns sexual?"

9. ***Will you meet me in real life?***

a. The online predator will ask to meet your child when he feels it is safe and he is sure your child will keep the meeting a secret.

b. The predator may ask the child to travel and provide money for a bus or plane ticket. City, state and country borders mean nothing to an online predator.

c. The online predator may get a hotel room near the meeting location or plan to molest the child in whatever vehicle the predator uses.

d. There is no timeframe for how quickly the meeting will take place. Earlier I told you about an online predator who requested the meeting for sex in the first instant message. I have also seen it take up to a year and a half for the online predator to feel safe enough to make all the arrangements. If the online predator lives in another country it may take longer because of the need to get airline tickets and visas. However, some online predators travel routinely from country to country and they may already have tickets and visas.

Question behind the question: "Will I get the opportunity to sexually molest you in person?"

10. ***Can you stay away from home for the whole night?***

a. An online predator may ask your child to spend the entire night in a motel with them.

b. They will ask your child to make up a story about staying at a friend's house, when in reality your child is meeting with the online predator. Know where your child is going and when. Do not rely on their friends' versions of sleepovers. Call and talk to their friends' parents to confirm a slumber party invitation.

Question behind the question: "How much time will I have to molest the child and then get far away from the scene before anyone starts looking for this child?" This can also mean: "If I am going to abduct this child, how long will it take before the child is going to be missed and a law enforcement agency is notified?"

III. Risky Behavior Online

There are certain activities that our children take part in that can increase the likelihood of coming into contact with an online predator. The federal government, via the Office of Juvenile Justice and Delinquency Prevention, the National Center for Missing and Exploited Children and the Crimes Against Children Research Center authored a study called *The Online Victimization of Youth: Five Years Later.* In this study, they discussed the online habits of our children, the effects of sexually explicit material available online and the interaction between children and online predators. The full study can be found at on the National Center for Missing and Exploited Children's website at http://www.missingkids.com/missingkids/servlet/ResourceServlet?LanguageCountry=en _US&PageId=2530.

The report identified numerous characteristics that our children display when they are online that may lead to contact with a sexual predator. I am only going to discuss a few here. If you want the full list, you can download a copy of the report from the website. There is no charge for downloading and printing a copy of the report.

Types of Risky Behavior:

- talking to people in various places online
- strangers added to buddy list
- talking to strangers about sex
- looking for pornographic content
- acting in a rude or nasty manner online
- harassing or posting embarrassing information about others online
- posting personal information in a profile, a blog or on a web page
- telling strangers your personal information
- use of file sharing programs for pornographic images

These are just some of the risky behaviors identified in the report. We will discuss them in a minute, but I think one that was not specifically addressed in the report needs to be included with this list. The most common trait we observe when called in by parents is *private computer use*. In nearly every instance in which we were called, the computer was in the child's bedroom or in a secluded location in the home. First and foremost, move the computer into a public area of the house. This makes secret contact on the computer more difficult.

Talking to People in Various Places Online

Children need boundaries to help keep them safe. You would not allow your child to go to just any neighborhood in any city in the world. Yet by letting them have unfiltered access to the internet, you are allowing them to visit some of the most dangerous and seedy neighborhoods in existence. Make sure your children understand where they are allowed go on the internet.

Strangers Added to Buddy List

Once children have a chat or instant message client, they feel the need to make sure they are "popular" within the community that uses that instant messaging client. To prove they are popular, they may add anyone and everyone who says hello to them online. Review your child's buddy list regularly and ask who each person on the buddy list is and how your child knows them. *Kick strangers off the buddy list and block them from returning.*

Talking to Strangers About Sex

This can be a tough one for most parents. Our children are using the internet to learn about sexual activity. In most cases, that education comes from online predators or people with very different ideas about sex and love. Fight through the embarrassment and talk to your children. Make sure they understand that degradation and pain is not part of a normal, caring or loving relationship.

Looking for Pornographic Content

Again, this one might mean fighting through some feelings of embarrassment, but explain that pornographic images are not indicative of a real or loving relationship. Some images are staged or posed, usually involving paid models. Other images of bestiality, torture or degrading acts are not proper conduct or content for your child.

Acting in a Rude or Nasty Manner Online

This is another one of those boundary issues. Children need to understand that just because they are in "cyberspace" it does not mean their actions will not have consequences. Rude or nasty comments may cause someone online to take offense and target them for retribution. This retribution may be conducted in a formal manner, such as a report to law enforcement that necessitates a police officer visiting their home. It could also be informal in that the child is barred from entering the chat, instant message or message board in the future. Most children need to know that when they are online they are not anonymous and their actions carry consequences.

Harassing or Posting Embarrassing Online

This is almost identical to the previous behavior, except that if the content posted online is in reference to race, creed, sex or violence, the content may actually be illegal. For example, if your child were to post information such as listing all the alternative lifestyle children in school, the result could be the risk of facing criminal charges. Regardless of whether or not the children listed were practicing truly alternative lifestyles, it can be considered a potential hate crime which is a criminal offense in some states. If the information threatens bodily harm or death, it would also be a criminal offense. Again, children need to understand that there are consequences to all of their actions online.

Also keep in mind that most school districts and state courts are ruling that content posted to the internet from a location off school property can still be within the disciplinary jurisdiction of the school. In other words, even though your child posted the information that disrupted school from your house, their friend's house or the public library, they can still be suspended or expelled from school.

Posting Personal Information in a Profile, a Blog or on a Web Page

At times, our children fill in whatever information is requested of them for a profile, blog or web page. They do not understand that providing your full name, address and date of birth can aid an online predator in finding them. It can also lead to the theft of their identity. Our children often do not understand that their identities can be just as valuable as those of their parents.

Telling Strangers Your Personal Information

When we talk to children at school, we learn that they understand that posting their real name, address and school name to an instant message profile can be dangerous. However, they do not realize that giving out that type of information during an instant message session can be just as dangerous. The reason they feel comfortable giving out the information during the grooming process is that the online predator has created an atmosphere of trust with your child. This atmosphere of trust causes our children to forget about the basic online safety rules. I will discuss this problem in greater detail in the section on instant messages and social networks.

If your child wants to create a profile, here is a list of information that is safe to include:

- Use a nickname only, not his or her real first or last name.
- Change the zip code to reflect one far from your hometown.
- If you are going to place images on the profile, use cartoons or drawings that show your child's interests.
- Never post images that identify your child, his or her school or hometown.
- Make the profile private and agree with your child in advance about who may be invited to see the profile.
- When your child wants to add another friend, make sure they know they must ask for your permission before adding anyone.

Use of File Sharing Programs for Pornographic Images

As technology changes and grows, our children are most often the first to embrace and use the new technology. One such technology is file sharing. Right now the legality of these programs is being fought in our courts. Our children use the file sharing networks to download all sorts of content. The most common downloads are MP3s. MP3s are audio files that are most commonly music files. The file sharing networks are full of millions of music files. When we speak with teachers and children the question that is asked most often is: "I downloaded the software and music for free, so why would that be illegal?" We try to explain why it is illegal to download music and movies without paying for the content.

As I mentioned in the Parental Control chapter of this book, one of the best ways to explain the complicated concept of copyright law to children is to compare the work that goes into creating a game like "Ages of Empire" or "Warcraft" to the work that they do when they study for a test. I explain that their high grade was their reward for their hard work and the children understand that they would not want to share their hard-earned grade with the entire class. Paying for video games and movies is how the musicians, actors and companies are rewarded for their hard work. The light bulbs start to go off over the children's heads and the questions usually change to: "If I pay for iTunes, Rhapsody or some other subscription service to download music and movies, is that legal downloading?" The measuring stick we leave them with is that if you are paying per file to download content or paying monthly fees, then you are probably legally obtaining content for your MP3 player.

IV. Instant Messages

Instant messages are private online communications between two users. The main difference between an instant message and a chat room is the privacy. Anything "posted" (geek for "said" or "typed") in the chat room can be seen by anyone in the chat room. In some chat rooms there can literally be thousands of users. So any message posted will be seen by thousands of people. This is not the preferred method of contact for an online predator. The instant message is the preferred tool of the online predator. They may "lurk" (enter a chat room but not engage in any conversations) waiting to see messages posted by a child that signal vulnerability. These signals can come in many forms: a fight with their parents, a bad grade at school, being harassed at school or just complaining about a bad day. Any information that gives the online predator an opening to approach your child in a sympathetic way can lead to a private conversation via an instant message.

However, this is not necessarily the approach every online predator will take. This subtle approach may take days or months for the online predator to build a secret relationship with your child. Some online predators will not be so patient and they will send an instant message asking the child personal questions from the very beginning.

At this point in an internet safety presentation, the parents usually ask, “Is one instant messaging client safer than the others?” Unfortunately, there is no completely safe instant messaging client. Some clients, like Yahoo! and America Online instant message (not to be confused with the America Instant Messenger Client), have taken steps to make their instant messaging clients safer. To this end, they look at the content of the chat room and do not allow certain types of chat rooms on their systems. America Online allows users to create chat rooms but have blocks against naming chat rooms for illegal content. I would not be allowed to create a chat room named "Preteen" because that room could be about trading images of children in sexual activity. These children would be under 13 years of age. The folks at America Online work hard to make the chat room area as safe as they can.

Yahoo! and Yahoo! Messenger took a different approach to make the chat rooms safer. They eliminated the ability for users to create their own chat rooms. Yahoo! has a set list of chat rooms and does not allow the creation of rooms that would center on victimizing children. They also ask the children their age when they sign up for an account and block anyone under the age of 18 from entering a chat room. By doing this, Yahoo! is helping to keep younger children out of chat rooms and away from online predators that may be lurking in there. Yahoo! also notifies each user via an instant message that their IP Address is being recorded. This means that Yahoo! has taken note of the IP Address used by each member and they keep a log of the IP Addresses. IP stands for "Internet Protocol," and each user online is assigned a specific IP Address for use as he or she navigates the internet, sends email, chats, sends instant messages or downloads content. Think of the IP Address as the house number of your home on the internet. Another way to look at the assigned IP Address is like the license plate on your vehicle. As you drive around the internet, this license plate travels with you and is registered for the date and time it was assigned to your computer. These dates and times are recorded in logs at your internet service provider. Law enforcement with the proper legal service (subpoena, search warrant or court order) can request the IP Address of a user who was reported for illegal contact or content. Via the IP Address, law enforcement can attempt to locate the predator using a screen name in an instant message, email, chat room, created profile or content posted to a blog. This is not a perfect system, but as you can see, most people's understanding of being "anonymous online" is incorrect. In fact, for many people, using the online format to molest children makes it easier for law enforcement to find them than if they were preying on children in the real world.

Some sites that cater specifically to children have now gone to a format where the children do not actually create the content that is viewed by another user. The children select from pre-approved phrases. They choose the phrase that most represents what they would like to say and then send it in an instant message. This format makes it very difficult, if not impossible, to elicit personal information or ask sexually oriented questions. I will discuss these sites in more detail in the next chapter.

While the folks at Yahoo! and America Online have tried to make their instant message clients and chat rooms safer, none of what they have done can prevent an online predator from entering a standard chat room. In fact, online predators will be drawn to wherever children congregate online, just as child predators in the real world are drawn to playgrounds, schools, malls and other physical locations frequented by children. They will search profiles to find the right sex, age and location of their next victim. Knowing this helps illustrate why your child should not list their age, sex or the name of their city in an online profile. (A comprehensive list of items which your child should know not to share is included in the Parental Control chapter of this book.) Any information in your child's profile that specifically separates them from all the other users can put them at risk.

Then, of course, there are other instant messaging clients built into free software programs that do not offer any protection to your children. This is where you need secondary filtering software installed on your computer to prohibit sexual content and the exchange of personal information.

Internet Relay Chat (IRC) has been around for a long time. It can be accessed via several free programs. Think of this chat area as the Wild West. No laws, very little law enforcement presence and an international mix of understanding as to what is legal or illegal. As I said earlier, if I was on America Online and attempted to create a chat room named "Preteen" I would receive a warning telling me the room name was illegal and that if I tried to create such a room again, my user account at America Online would be terminated. This is not an idle threat; they are serious about protecting children and they would terminate my user account.

Here is just a brief list of some of the chat rooms available via IRC. At the time I took this screen capture there were over 30,000 chat rooms created on this set of servers for IRC.

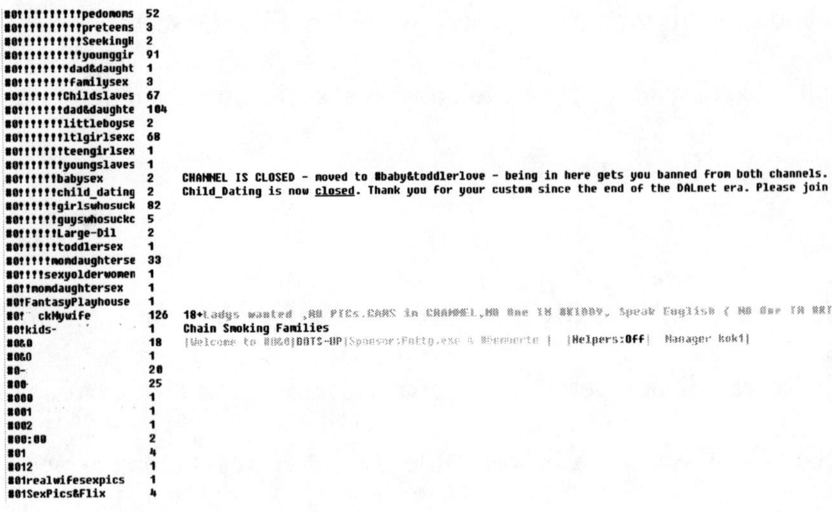

As you can see from the list of names, some of the rooms would not be allowed on most of the other instant messaging clients. The second room is “Preteen” and it is joined by “Babysex” and “Toddlersex.” Yes, babies and toddlers are the focus of the room. Or, more specifically, having sex with or documenting sexual activity with babies and toddlers via digital photographs or video is the focus of the rooms. Every day law enforcement is confronted with larger numbers of images and movies. Some of the movies come complete with the sound of infants (under one year old) and toddlers (two to three years old) being molested.

The study *Internet Sex Crimes Against Minors: The Response of Law Enforcement* by the National Center for Missing and Exploited Children, the Office of Juvenile Justice and Delinquency Prevention and the Crimes Against Children Research Center showed that almost 20% of the children shown in the images received by law enforcement were less than three years of age.

In this example, I am using the instant messenger client from Yahoo! (this does not mean Yahoo! Messenger is any better or worse then any other instant message client). Your child would create a user account, and in this example the user account is in the name of Tracies123321. In fact, my **Personal Favorites** are **Yahoo! Messenger** and **America Online Instant Messenger (AIM)**. I can use them to keep in touch with my children when they are away at college or busy at work.

You can see the name at the top part of the messenger interface. Once I add a friend, the screen name of the friend will appear in the large open rectangle below Tracies' name. If this child had created a profile, an online predator would probably check it out for additional information before making contact. The online predator might learn from the profile where the child lives, what grade they are in or what band is their favorite. All of that information is perfect for formulating a strategy to make an online approach. In this example, the online predator using the screen name johnbadguy1 says hello to Tracie by using IMing shorthand language.

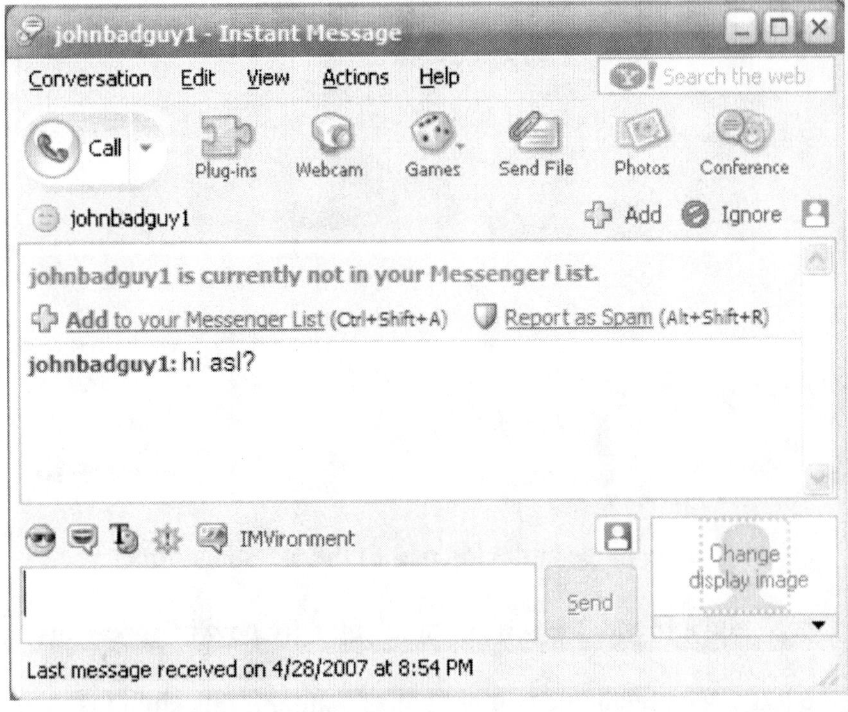

ASL is shorthand for "Age, Sex, Location." What johnbadguy1 is asking Tracie is how old she is, what gender she is and where she lives. There are many shortcuts used for chatting and IMing. If you want to see what shorthand language means, try typing "chat language" or "chat abbreviations" into Google and you will find many sites that will help you understand the shorthand language.

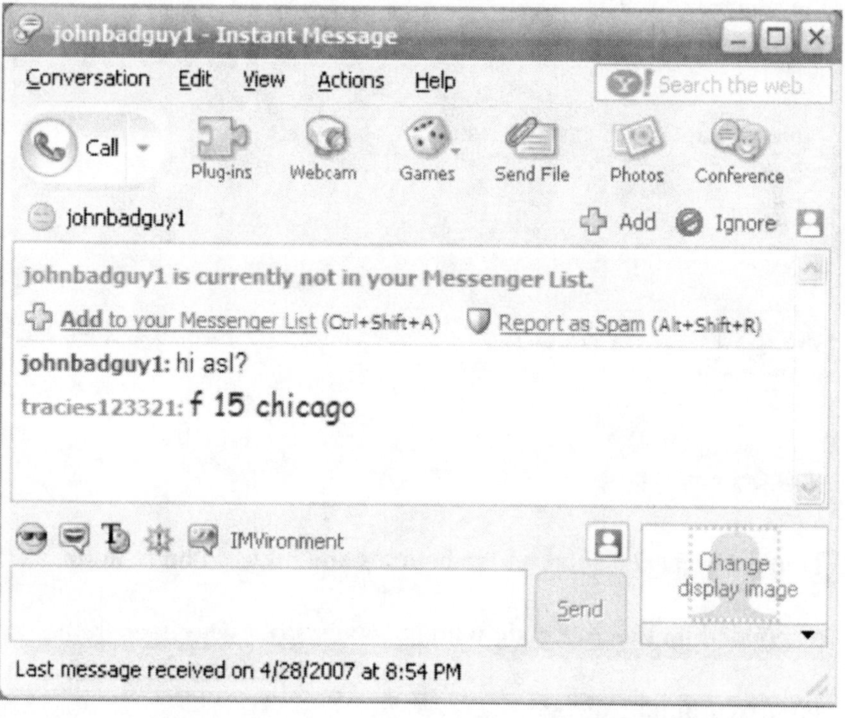

Tracie responds saying she is a female who is 15 years of age and lives in Chicago.

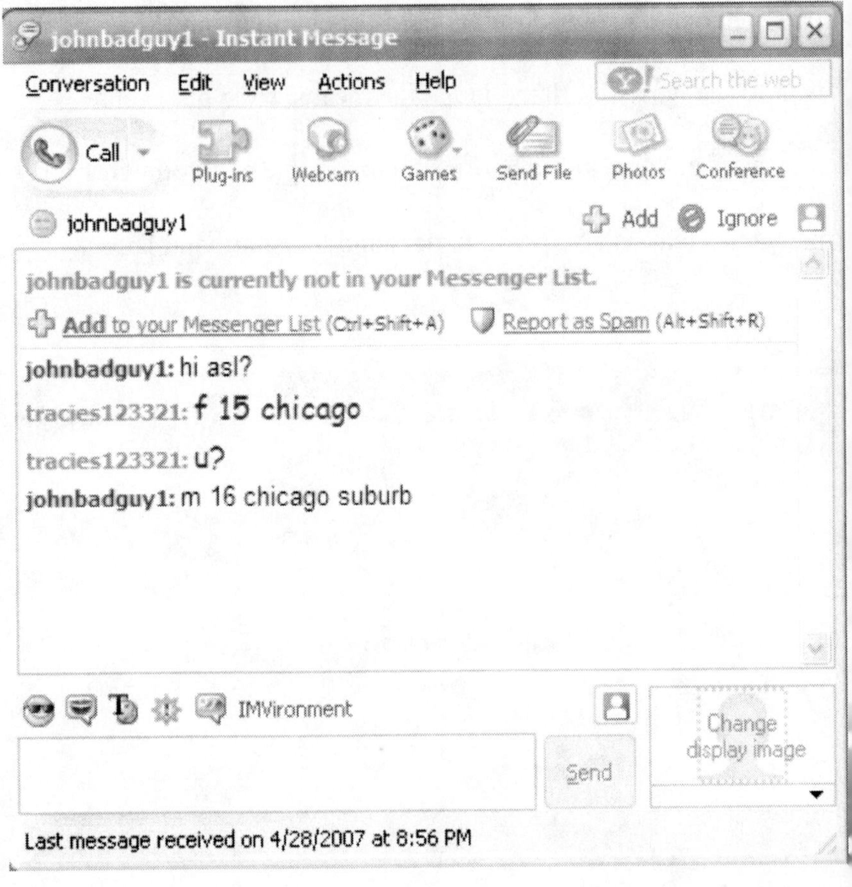

Tracie then asked John where he lives and how old he is. John responded that he is a male who is 16 years old who lives in the suburbs around Chicago.

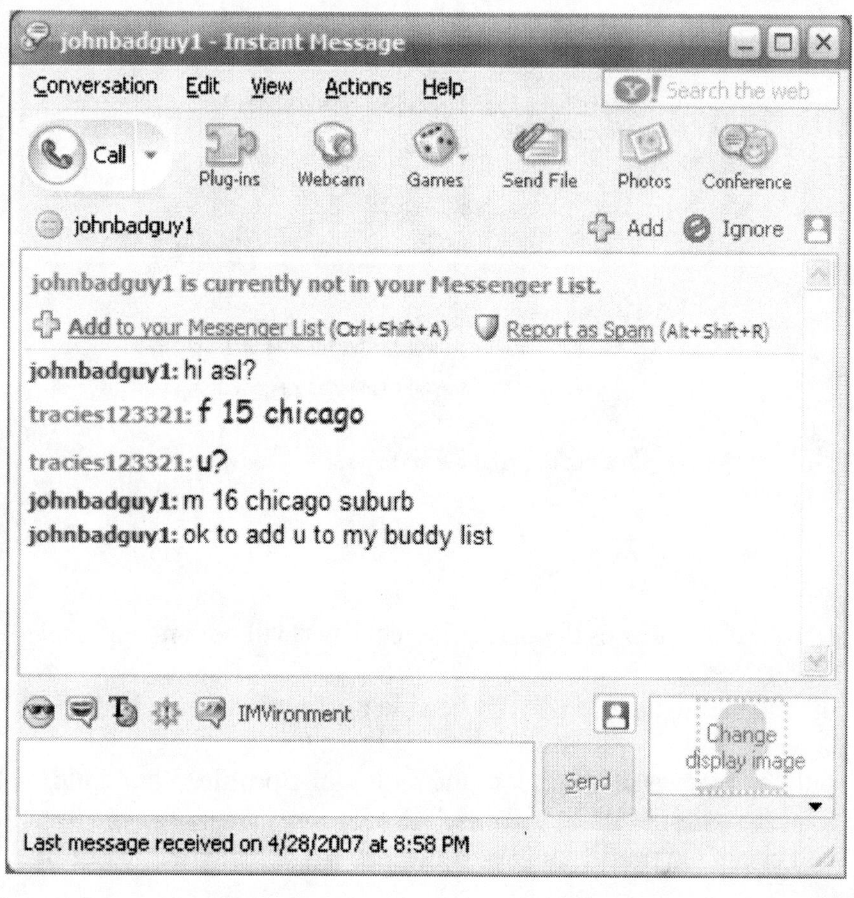

John is asking to be added to Tracie's buddy list. If Tracie allows John to be added to her buddy list, he may learn some personal information about Tracie. You must send a request to be added to a buddy list, but the other user gets an opportunity to accept or refuse the offer.

Add to Messenger List Request

John Bad (johnbadguy1) would like to add you to his or her Messenger List as tracies123321.

View this person's profile

What do you want to do?

- ◉ Allow this person to add me and see when I am online
  - ☑ And add this person to my Messenger List
- ○ Do not allow this person to add me or see when I am online

If your child refuses the offer, the requester will not only be kept off the buddy list but will not be able to see when your child is online. There is also a link to the requestor's profile. Your child can check the profile and see if there is any content on the profile that says, "Do not add this person." What kind of content would say, "Do not add?" Well, for instance, a nude image of the predator on his profile, or the predator saying he is only 16 in the instant message, but on his profile he lists his age as 50 years old.

A second warning screen tells your child that if they allow the predator to add them to their buddy list, the predator will see some personal information.

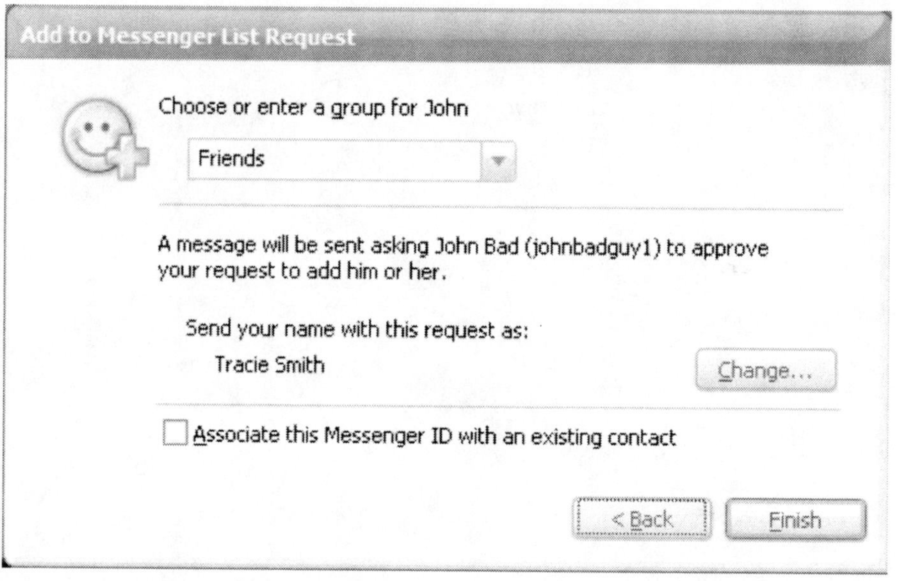

The warning shows that once you allow your screen name to be added to the predator's buddy list, they will see your full name. In this example, the name entered when Tracie created her account was Tracie Smith.

Now instead of seeing the screen name “Tracies123321” on the predator’s buddy list, he sees her first and last name. This information is picked up from when the account was created.

About this time, parents want to know who the online predators are going after, and what age children they are trying to contact. Most of the contact I have seen is with children between the sixth and ninth grades. They prefer children who are between the ages of 11 to 14 but will go up as high as 16 years of age. These children are old enough to communicate on the computer and are reaching out for contact beyond their family. Children at this age suffer from their curiosity outweighing their maturity. They are just starting to become involved in activities outside of their home. Because of those activities, they have times when they are unsupervised by parents or teachers. That free time is what the online predators are trying to control.

Any parent of a junior high school student can tell you how vulnerable children are at that age. Children at this age seem to have lost the ability to recognize there is a world outside of their own existence. I know at my house, it seemed as if I was constantly reminding them to pay attention and try to focus. They could not remember homework assignments. We were constantly going back to school to retrieve forgotten text books and there was only half a chance that any items they left the house with would actually return home. After speaking to parents of other children, I learned our children were no different than most of the children in junior high.

I realized that with everything that is going on in a child's life during this stage, they make the perfect targets. They are trying to adjust to the differences between elementary school and a junior high. They are now old enough to be unsupervised at times, yet not mature enough to be prudent with that unsupervised time. Now, add to the mix some raging hormones and you can see why these children are the preferred targets of the online predator. All of this chaos makes these children easy prey.

The raging hormones and natural curiosity bring the children into contact with the online predators. Our children want to have friends and an existence outside of their family. This need to have friends is used by online predators in the grooming of our children. You can see why having filtering or logging programs installed on your computer is so important. With the proper filtering program installed, your child would not be able to enter the chat rooms in

IRC. With the filters set properly, your children could not even load the names of the chat rooms without the filtering program alerting you to the prohibited content and shutting off the offending program. The online grooming process needs an atmosphere of secrecy to be successful. Filtering and key logging programs can give you the necessary information in the form of user names, passwords and accounts created by your child to help you identify risky behavior and help you protect your child.

When you understand the intent of the online predator and vulnerability of the children you can see the predatory nature of these criminals.

V. Blogs and Online Journals

Most parents do not understand what a blog is and why their children would want to have one or post information there. The term "blog" is a mixture of the words "web page" and "log." A blog is simply an online diary that allows children to speak their minds about what is happening in their lives. The problem is that blogs are web pages. Let me say that again, *blogs are web pages and web pages are not private*. Most of the children who create blogs do so with the notion that any content they add to the blog will only be seen by the friends they allow onto their blog. This is not true; a blog is like any other web page and may become available for anyone on the internet to read.

When someone has a diary, they usually keep the diary under lock and key. The last thing they want is for strangers (or worse, parents) to read their diary. However, put that diary online and it magically becomes cool to have everyone in the world reading your most personal thoughts.

So, the main problem with blogs is that our children enter their most personal thoughts there and do not realize who will read them. Some children will enter their real name, complain about how boring their city is and how they are having a bad time in school. While this may be cathartic for the child, it is dangerous and pure gold for the online predator. Predators are looking for a way into your child's life. What better way to gain entry into your child's life than to be that sympathetic voice consoling your child about their boring city or rough time in school? The online predator will try to let your child know that things will get better in high school or college and that everyone hates junior high school or high school. They will explain how one good friend can help you through the rough times. Of course the online predator would like to apply for the job of that one good friend.

Blogs can be created all by themselves or in conjunction with other sites. Social networking sites may include profiles, blogs, music and images. In the next chapter I will talk about social networking sites in more detail. Treat a blog like a profile. Explain to your child how personal information in a blog can be as dangerous as putting the same personal information in a profile. Make sure your child understands that even if the site claims that the online journal or blog is private, it is a web page and web pages are not private.

VI. Texting

Texting is something parents have a little more control over right now, because for most services there is a charge for texting. Some have a flat rate and others charge per text message. When my son started getting into texting with his friends, we noticed the constant typing of messages on his cell phone. His friends preferred texting to a phone conversation, probably because most of them were either at work or school where they could not have a conversation but could still text. In fact, my son got so good at it he did not have to look at his phone to be able to type a text message. Well, it is not as if text messages are written with proper spelling and grammar.

Our first effort to curtail the texting was to tell him to stop. We could tell by the increase in the bill the texting did not stop. We confronted him and he explained it was not his fault. "Mom and Dad, I stopped, but my friends keep sending them so you keep getting charged." My wife came up with a perfect solution to that problem. Whatever the monthly charge was for the texting portion of the bill, my son had to pay his mother that amount from his paycheck from his after-school job. Once he had to pay for the texting messages himself, they decreased drastically. He has gone back to instant messaging and emailing friends instead of texting.

The major issue with texting is the secrecy of the messages and the ability of the online predator to use texting in concert with telephone calls. If the online predator can text your child, he probably has your child's cell phone number. Once the online predator has voice communication with your child, the grooming process speeds up. It is much easier and quicker to groom a child when you can talk to them, rather than just typing messages to them.

Some systems actually retain the text messages and they can be downloaded and reviewed. If you notice a spike in your texting bill, you may want to see if the messages are recorded and find out whom your child is texting.

CHAPTER 4: SOCIAL NETWORKING SITES

I. What Is a Social Network?

Social networking on the internet is a relatively new phenomenon that has caught on with children of all ages. These networking sites allow our children to create profiles, add music, photos, videos and blogs to create a personalized version of a web page. Every year, the age of children using computers is getting younger and younger. I am not talking about using computers to play simple games or for learning the alphabet. Our children are using the computer to research homework assignments in the third grade. They are using computers as a regular part of school in the first grade. By the fourth or fifth grade, most children are using programs like Microsoft's Word for text, PowerPoint for slide shows and Front Page to design web pages. Knowing this, you can understand why social networking sites became so popular so quickly with our children. It allowed them to use the skills learned at school and inject their own personality to create a web page that announces their presence to the world. In a perfect world, these announcements would be a great way for the children to express themselves and interact with eachother. However, we live in a world that is far from perfect.

I have worked in computer crime investigation long enough to know that the uproar over these new sites brings about a familiar ring from days past. Right now, everyone is up in arms over the fact that children are posting personal information to these profiles, which may cause them to have contact with online predators. The type of uproar is reminiscent of the old Frankenstein movies where the town-folk take up arms and storm the castle, looking to kill the monster. This is not the first time I have seen the townfolk storm a cyber castle.

About ten years ago, when America Online and MSN first launched, they allowed children to create profiles using personal information. At first, the sites suggested what content the children might want to add to a profile. They had place markers for their first, middle and last name. There was a box to check gender. Next, the children would enter their date of birth and age. The next few boxes dealt with where they lived and included the name of their city and state. Children could list hobbies, personal comments and talk about things they liked to do online as well as in the real world.

The online predators realized how this system could be "searched" and how the search engines could be used to find their next victim. Remember earlier, when I told you about the online predator who would fly around the country and use the online system to search for his next victim? Well, online predators would go to the list of profiles and use the search engine to list the type of child they preferred to molest.

If you understand an online predator's concept of a search engine, it becomes clear how to misuse the search features. An online predator would simply enter the age and gender of their preferred victim and allow the system to search all the profiles. If, for instance, I knew I would be flying to Chicago, Illinois, I could add that parameter to the search request. Now the search engine would be looking for a child's profile that matched the specific gender, age and geographical location I entered.

Law enforcement met with America Online and MSN and explained how the search engines were being used to victimize children. In time the age, city and gender boxes were removed from the profiles. Since this was all new, no one realized how the information was going to be misused. However, once the vulnerabilities were explained the companies not only removed the requests for this type of information, they started posting safety tips for filling out profiles. Children were cautioned against using their real names or giving out any personal information and were given methods to report unwanted contact immediately.

Armed with this knowledge, the profiles our children created were safer. In fact, today when we ask children during an internet safety training how many have an instant message client almost all the children raise their hands. When we ask about information posted to a profile they respond, “Just my screen name, not my real name.” They do not list the city they live in or the school they attend. In fact, the internet safety training seems to be getting through to the children when it comes to chat rooms and instant messaging. They are listening and they are creating safer profiles for instant message clients.

However, it is an altogether different story when we ask about the profile they created on a social networking site. They listed their first, middle and last name. They listed their gender, full dates of birth and their home address. Why the big difference between instant message profiles and social networking sites? I believe there are two reasons for the very different behaviors. First, some social networking sites use a form asking all the basic questions about your name, age, gender, home address and likes and dislikes. Our children feel compelled to fill out this form in its entirety. The second reason is that the children “feel” safer on the social networking sites. They view social networking sites as “their” dominion and don't believe online predators use these sites the same way they use instant message clients.

There are many social networking sites. MySpace, Facebook, Friendster, Xanga and Club Penguin are just a few of the sites online. I am not saying any of these sites are safer than any other site. I am not saying that any of these sites are more dangerous than the others. *The fact is the sites are not always the problem.* I know that last statement is a controversial statement at best. Most articles on television or in the newspapers tend to blame the sites for any illegal conduct. However, most of the time it is the content posted by our children that caused the problem. I know it is easier to blame the website, social networking site or online predator for what happened, but the fact is, our children and we as parents must accept some of the responsibility. When a drunk driver causes an accident that kills someone, we do not blame the vehicle or the vehicle manufacturer. We blame the driver. In some regards, this logic needs to be applied to the phenomenon of social networking sites. We must correct the posting habits of our children, the responsibility of parents to monitor their child's activities on line and the need for site owners to make the sites as safe as possible.

One day at home my wife said, "You know you are always teaching *other* children how to be safe online. What about taking some time to look at your child's social networking site and making sure *he* is safe?" That one stung a little bit, but she was right. I sat down with my son and went through his site. It just happened to be a MySpace page. If I had to pick a favorite social networking site, I would have to say: **Personal Favorite Social Networking Site: MySpace.**

Why would I pick MySpace over the others? I like their willingness to work with law enforcement, to change anything they feel may be dangerous and the lengths they take to locate and remove sexual predators from their site.

As my son and I reviewed his MySpace I would point out what I felt might be dangerous to him. First, he had entered his full name.

I asked why he entered his full name and he replied, "Because the site asked for my first, middle and last name." I explained to him he did not have to enter his full name and that it would be safer to enter a nickname. He asked me how his friends could find his MySpace profile if all he did was enter a nickname? I asked him, "How do your friends find your profile now?" He said, "I have to tell them what name to search for on MySpace." I asked him if it would be a big deal to search for his nickname instead of his first or last name. He looked at me and said it wouldn't really matter because most of his friends call him by his nickname anyway. At this point, he realized changing the name wouldn't affect his friends' ability to find his site.

My son listed his full date of birth and home address. I explained to him how having his full name, date of birth and address listed could lead him to being a victim of identity theft. He was supplying thieves with all the information they needed to create a false identity using his information. At this point, we removed the date of birth and address.

As we went through the rest of the profile, he did pretty well. However, when we went through his answers to the survey we hit a snag. The survey is composed of 80 questions that ask users to enter their personal preferences for music, food, restaurants and beverages. Most of this information was harmless, until we got to the question, "Have you ever broken the law?" My son had checked "Yes." Remember earlier when I said children will not confide in you if you overreact? Well, here I am, a police officer, and my son has checked that he has broken the law. Having my teenage son tell me he broke the law caused my mind to run amuck thinking about what he might have done. I managed to refrain from strangling my son and asked, "What have you done?" My son replied, "Well, Dad, sometimes I drive without my seatbelt." Now I am not making light of not wearing a seatbelt, but I have to admit that what crossed my mind was, "If this is as bad as my rebel son has been, then my wife has done a great job of raising him."

When we teach internet safety to children and parents, we try to explain that information in a MySpace profile can lead to contact with online predators. Look at the profile and see if any of the information there might cause your child to stand out from the 220 million other users on MySpace.

How does your child create a MySpace account? It is as easy as launching a browser and typing in www.myspace.com.

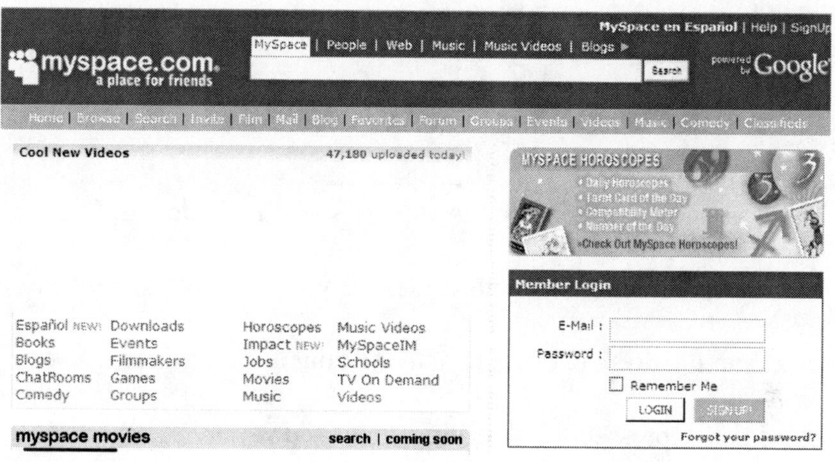

To create a MySpace account click on *Sign Up*.

Home | Browse | Search | Invite | Film | Mail | Blog | Favorites | Forum | Groups | Events | Videos | Music | Comedy | Classifieds

Already a member? **Click Here to Log In**

JOIN MYSPACE HERE!

Please enter a valid e-mail address. You will need to confirm your e-mail address to activate your account.

Email Address:

First Name:

Last Name:

Password:

Confirm Password:

Country: United States

Postal Code:

Date Of Birth: Month Day Year

Gender: Female Male

Allow others to see when it's my birthday

Preferred Site & Language: U.S.A.

By checking the box you agree to the MySpace Terms of Service and Privacy Policy.

Sign Up

Why Join MySpace?

» Create a Custom Profile
» Upload Pictures
» Send Mail and IM's
» Write Blogs & Comments
» It's **FREE**!

MySpace understands that user privacy is the key to our success.

Already a member?

Please read our privacy policy.

The first thing that you need to supply is an email address. In reading the directions you notice it says you will have to confirm your email address in order to activate your account. I have also heard this expressed as "verifying email addresses." This can be a misleading concept. To create a MySpace account all I need to do is fill in the information requested complete with an email address. That does not mean they are verifying that I am who I said I am. That does not mean they have verified who was sitting at the keyboard typing in the information. All it means is that I supplied an email address that was active. In this example, I supplied an email address from a free Yahoo! account. Before signing up for the MySpace account, I went to Yahoo! and created the email address I was going to use for creating the account at MySpace.

Home | Browse | Search | Invite | Film | Mail | Blog | Favorites | Forum | Groups | Events | Videos | Music | Comedy | Classifieds

Already a member? Click Here to Log In

JOIN MYSPACE HERE!

Please enter a valid e-mail address. You will need to confirm your e-mail address to activate your account.

Email Address: tracies123321@yahoo com
First Name: Tracie
Last Name: Smith
Password: ••••••••••
Confirm Password: ••••••••••
Country: United States
Postal Code: 60601
Date Of Birth: January 1 1980
Gender: Female Male
Allow others to see when it's my birthday
Preferred Site & Language: U.S.A.
By checking the box you agree to the MySpace Terms of Service and Privacy Policy.
Sign Up

Why Join MySpace?
» Create a Custom Profile
» Upload Pictures
» Send Mail and IM's
» Write Blogs & Comments
» It's **FREE**!

MySpace understands that user privacy is the key to our success.
Already a member?
Please read our privacy policy.

I submitted the email address of tracies123321@yahoo.com and provided the first and last name for the account. Additional information requested is the user's zip code, date of birth, gender, preferred site and language. The date of birth is used to set the parameters of the account. In other words, children under 18 have limitations on how they can search or be searched.

We will come back to the use of the zip code a little later.

After checking the box that you agree to the terms of service, click on the *Sign Up* button and you can begin to customize your MySpace profile.

Upload Some Photos!

The second step in creating your profile is sharing your photos to let friends and other members see who you are.

Photos may be a max of 600K in these formats: GIF or JPG [help]

Photos may not contain nudity, violent or offensive material, or copyrighted images. If you violate these terms, your account will be deleted. [photo policy]

If you don't see the Upload Photo form below, click **here**

Upload Photo

Browse...

Upload

Skip for now

By clicking on the *Browse* button you can search your hard drive or any other storage media for an image that you want displayed on your site. Find the image, click on the image, click on *Upload* and the image appears on your MySpace page.

One thing to keep in mind is that all MySpace profiles are reviewed for content. They try to get to each profile within a very short time span. If you uploaded nude images to your profile it will cause your profile to be deleted.

Next, you can announce to all your friends that your MySpace is ready for visitors.

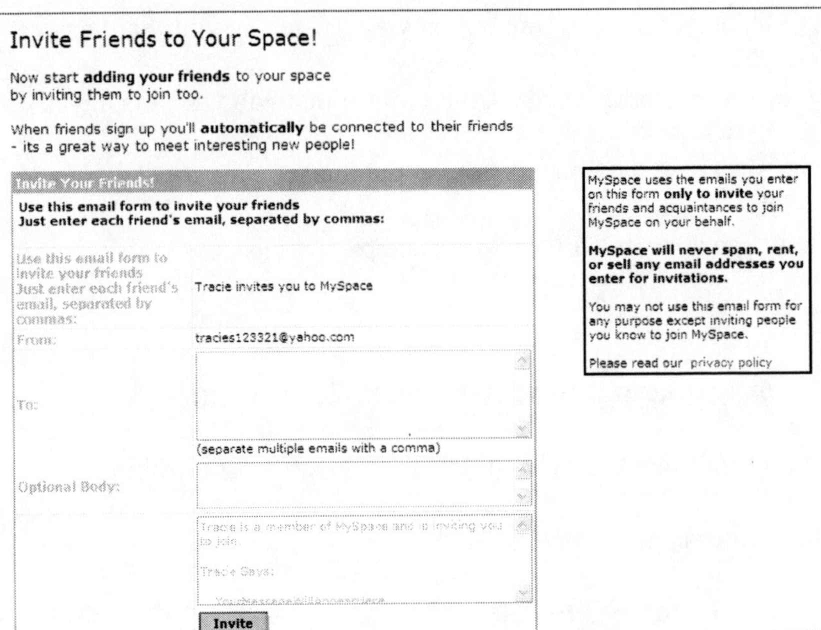

Type in the email addresses of all the friends you want to invite to view your profile and MySpace will send out a notification complete with a link to your profile.

After sending the invitations you can visit your MySpace home page.

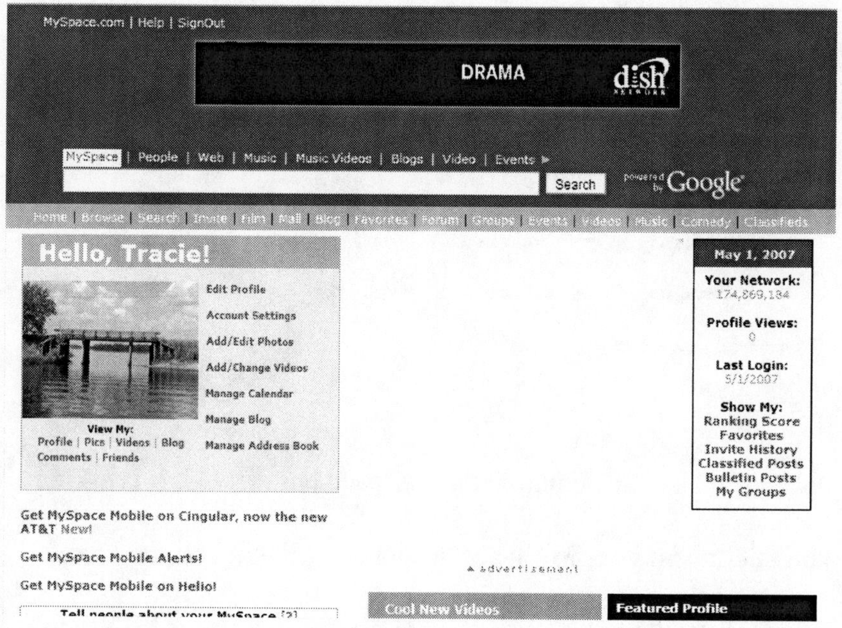

At this time you might want to go to the email address you supplied when you created the account and see if the verification/activation email has arrived.

To: tracies123321@yahoo.com
Date: 1 May 2007 13:17:38 -0700
Subject: MySpace Account Confirmation

Hi Tracie -- Thanks for joining MySpace!

Here's your account info for logging in:

E-mail:
Password:

Keep it secret. Keep it safe.

Please confirm your MySpace account by clicking here:

http://collect.myspace.com/reloc.

======================

We hope you're having fun on the site. Have you checked out these areas yet?

* MUSIC - listen and download music from great new bands right on the site!

http://music.myspace.com/

As you can see, the email from MySpace has arrived. It is asking you to confirm your MySpace account by clicking on the link. If you click on the link your browser will open and your MySpace home page will be displayed.

Obviously, I am not "Tracie." I set up an email address by that name on a free email site. I used the address when filling out the forms for Tracie's MySpace page. I received the email from MySpace asking me to confirm the email address by clicking on the activation link. The only thing verified here is that the email address I supplied is active. It did not verify that I am Tracie. It did not verify that Tracie is a real person, or for that matter, that Tracie was actually a female.

MySpace is trying to take additional steps to limit false accounts and I applaud their efforts, but I want to make sure that parents understand the terms verification or verifying email addresses as used here do not mean verifying who is at the keyboard. Currently, I do not know of any way that you can be 100% certain who is sitting at the keyboard when an account is created or someone is chatting.

Once I have a MySpace account, I can then customize it. I can add comments by clicking on *Edit Profile*. I can add comments about what I like doing, what grade I am attending or my age. The age entered in this location is not verified against the date of birth entered on the previous screen.

About Me:

Preview Section | Preview Profile

I'd Like to Meet:

Preview Section | Preview Profile

Interests:

Preview Section | Preview Profile

Music:

A user can enter anything they like in these fields and it will appear on their MySpace profile. Again, it will not be verified with any other information provided during the creation of the account.

Your child can continue the customization by adding images, movies and songs. The movies and songs can be found on MySpace and linked to your child's profile.

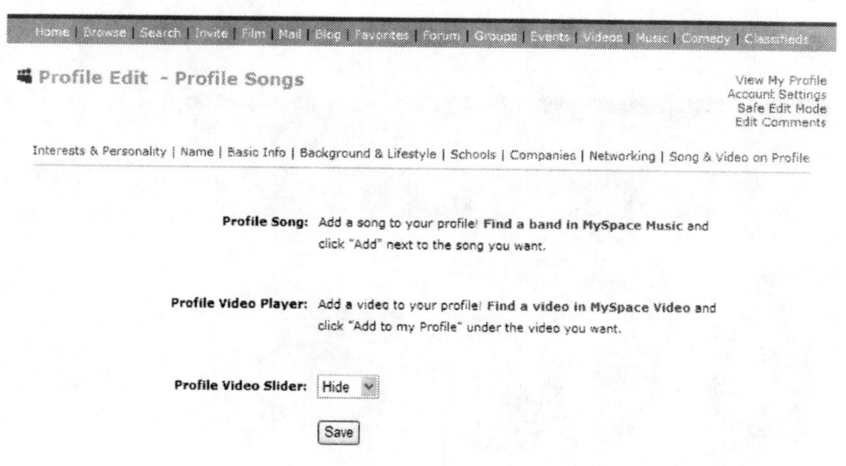

To add a song, click on *Edit Profile* and then on *Music*. In this example, I selected a band that could be found on MySpace. The link took me to a page where I could select from hundreds of bands and thousands of songs. After selecting a song, simply click *Add* and then *Upload* and now when people visit your MySpace they will hear that song.

Next, your child will add a blog to their MySpace. This blog will be an online communication between your child and his or her friends. Each can post messages to the blog. It ends up being a running commentary on what is happening in your child's life.

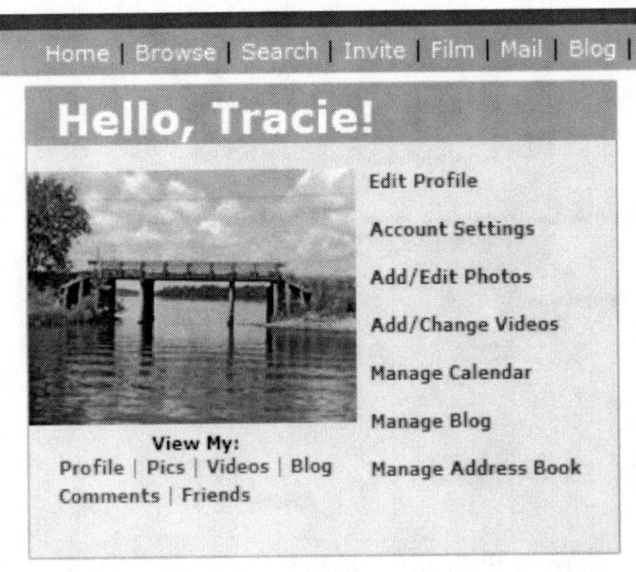

In this example, the blog is located at http://blog.myspace.com/traciesmith123321 and the MySpace is located at http://www.myspace.com/traciesmith123321. Your child can send these links to their friends in an email address. Their friends can visit your child's MySpace or their blog by clicking on the link in an email.

Children are being taught how to create web pages at school in an environment where they are protected by the teacher, the filtering programs installed by the school and the fact that they only have access to limited content. Once they leave school they have all the knowledge to create a MySpace profile but not necessarily all the maturity needed to do it safely. That is where you come in. Sit down with your child and review their work. Compliment the good, help to understand and change the not-so-good. Do not loose sight of the fact that your children may be very proud of their MySpace page. The skills it takes to create the site will help them in school and ultimately in the work place. Help them use these skills correctly.

I am frequently asked if it is better to allow my child to have a MySpace profile or to deny them access to such content. As a parent, I have learned to pick my battles. When it comes to the computer, I think it is better to work with your child and create as safe a profile as possible. If you challenge your child by denying them access to these sites, sooner or later as they grow older they will find a way around you. They will learn to keep their profiles a secret, and secrets play right into the hands of online predators. I tell parents during my internet safety presentations that my son has a MySpace profile and how we worked together to make it as safe as possible when he was younger and lived at home. Now he is away at college. He still has his MySpace profile and now he has full control of it. We had the time between when he was approximately eight years old until he was 18 to instill the proper morals and values in our son. After 18 he was off to college where there were no limits on his internet use. I think it is better to let your children learn responsibility a little bit at a time while they still live at home so that they are prepared when all the controls and support are removed when they turn 18 and move out.

II. How Does an Online Predator Use a Social Network?

Think back to how the instant messaging online predator used the search tools of the profile system to help locate his next victim. Social networks resurrected the problem. Their search programs can be used by an online predator to locate any child by age, sex and location. For the next demonstration, we are going to think like an online predator and use the search engine just as an online predator would.

In this example, we are using MySpace, but this can be done on any system that allows the following types of searches.

First sign onto MySpace and click on the *Search* tab.

Home | Browse | Search | Invite | Film | Mail | Blog |

This will open up the different search fields. The first search we will use is the school search.

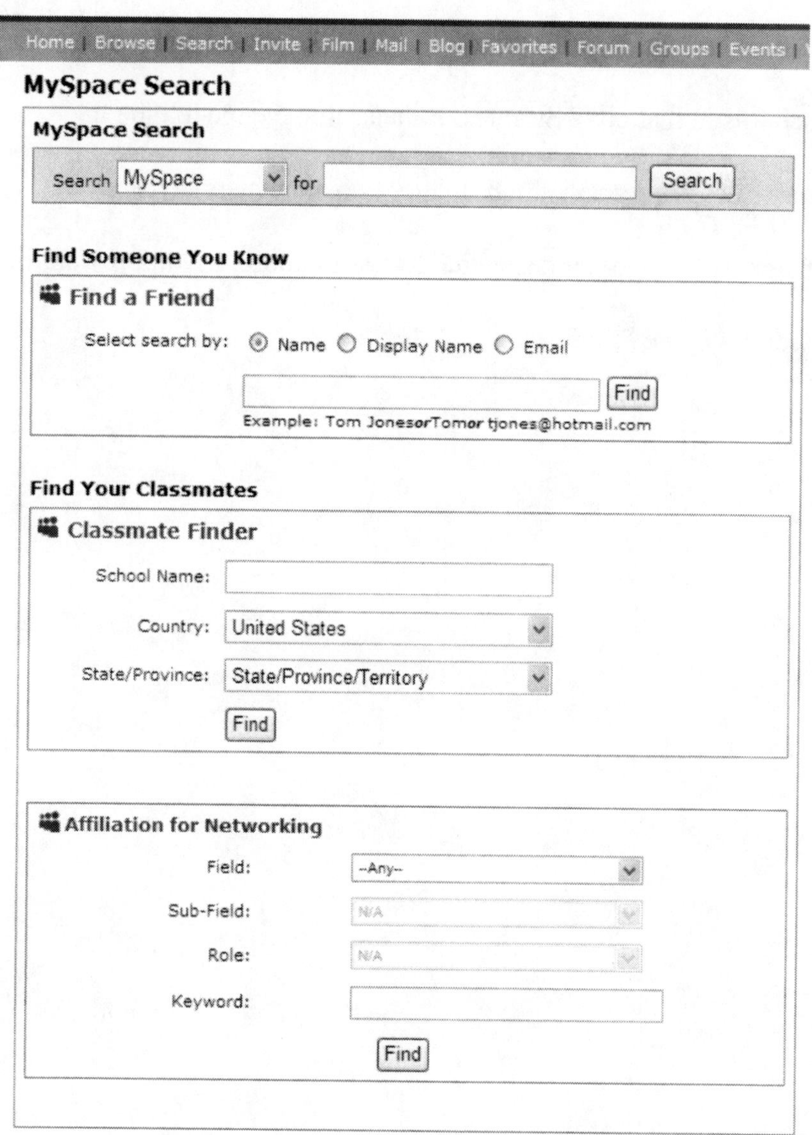

The middle search is called the *Classmate Finder* and allows us to search for MySpace profiles via the school name associated with the profile. If I know what city I will be traveling to, I can search the schools in that city. What if I do not know the name of the schools in that city? Simple, let the search engine tell me the names of the schools. First, I enter two characters in the school name. It does not matter which letters I choose, because I want the search engine to fail.

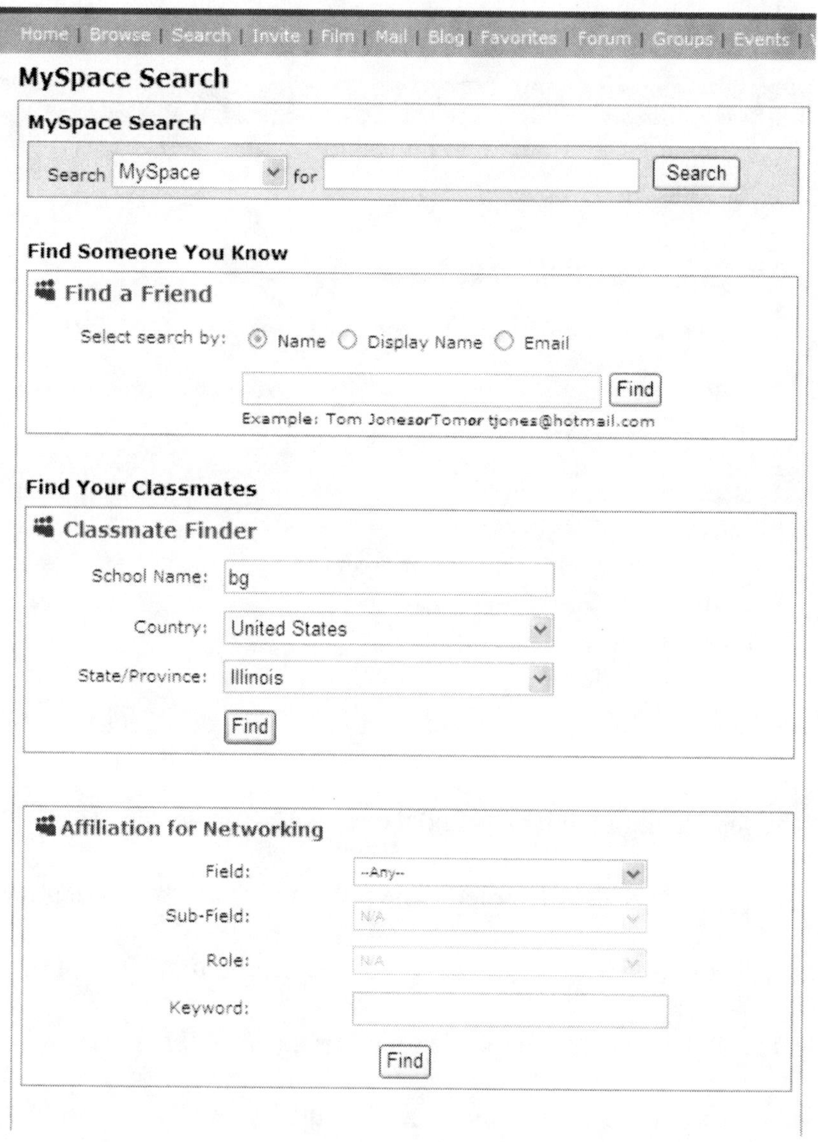

I entered the characters "bg" for the school name and selected the state I will be traveling to in the near future. Click on *Find*.

Search Schools

No schools were found.

1. **Try locating your school by the city**
   Select The First Letter of the City of Your School:

   A B C D E F G H I J K L M N O P Q R S T U V W X Y Z

Or:

2. **Try searching again:**

Find a Classmate

School Name: bg

Country: United States

State/Province: Illinois

Find

The search engine failed to find the school by name and is now letting us know that if we let it know what city we are looking for, it will continue to hunt for the school. Select the first letter of the name of the city we will be visiting. For this example I know I will be visiting Naperville, Illinois. To find the list of city names beginning with “N” and the city of Naperville, click on the letter *N*.

Home | Browse | Search | Invite | Film | Mail | Blog | Favorites | Forum | Groups | Events | Videos

Search Schools

Illinois > Select Your School's City:

A B C D E F G H I J K L M N O P Q R S T U V W X Y Z

Nachusa
Naperville
Naperville-nor
Nashville
Nauvoo
Nelson
Neoga
Neponset
New Athens
New Baden
New Berlin
New Boston
New Douglas
New Lenox
Newark
Newman
Newton
Niantic
Niles
Noble
Nokomis
Normal
Norridge
Norris City
North Aurora
North Chicago
North Riversid
North Riverside
Northbrook
Northfield
Northlake

To get a list of the different grade levels of schools in Naperville, Illinois, click on *Naperville*.

Home | Browse | Search | Invite | Film | Mail | Blog | Favorites |

Search Schools

Illinois > Naperville > Select Your Grade Level:

High School (9-12)
Elementary Through High School (1-12)
Jr. High Through High School (6-12)
College/University
Trade School

View All Schools In This City

Now select the level of school or, as online predators would do, select the age of the child they are looking to victimize. Since their primary focus would be on junior high school students, click on *Jr. High through High School.*

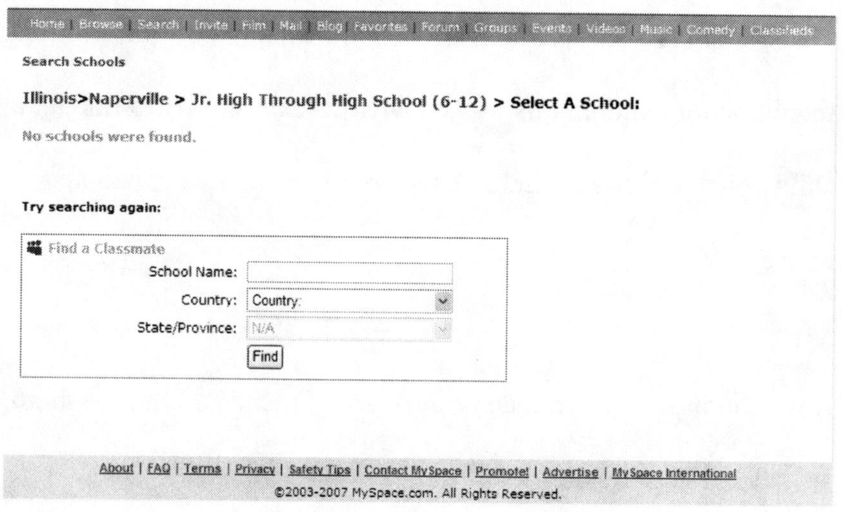

If you believe the search engine, then there are apparently no junior high schools in the city of Naperville. This is not true, of course, as there are multiple junior high schools in Naperville, Illinois.

When I said I would choose **MySpace** as my **Personal Favorite** it was qualified by two reasons. The first is that they are constantly trying to make the site safer. The second is they are willing to listen to and work with law enforcement. Just like in the past when the internet service providers learned that putting age, sex and home city location in profiles was dangerous and removed those fields, when law enforcement noticed the same issue with searching for children this way on MySpace the ability to find a child younger than high school age was removed by the people at MySpace.

If we continue the search and select *High School* you can see there are several high schools listed in Naperville, Illinois.

In this example, I selected *Neuqua Valley High School*.

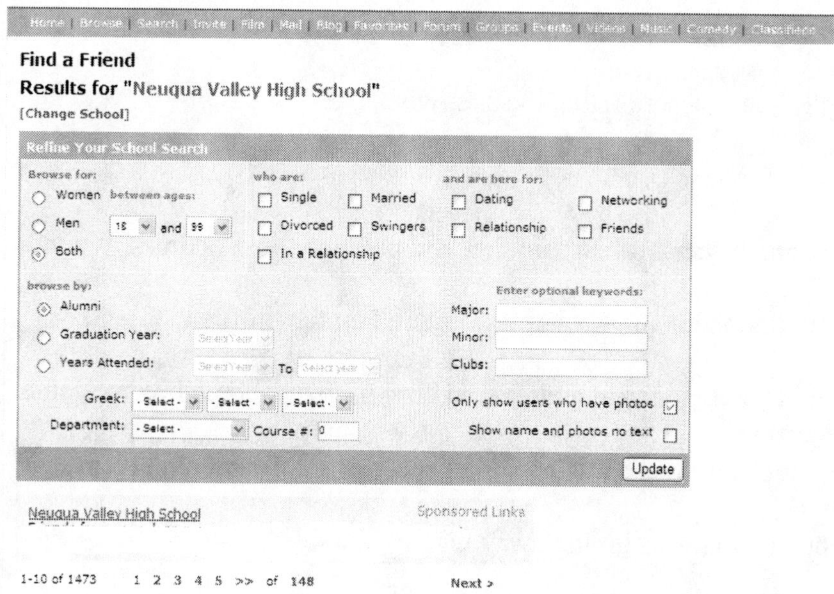

The search engine let me know there are 1,473 MySpace profiles associated with Neuqua Valley High School. That does not mean they are all current high school students or even students. Some of the people in the profiles may be in college now, and others might be teachers or other employees at the school.

The school search is not the only way children might be at risk on a social networking site. Remember, we are teaching our children not to put their address in a profile. However, when I spoke with children during internet safety training, I learned that they did list their address in social networking sites. They felt a need to enter all the information that the site requested.

Some of the children said they did not enter their address. When I queried them about what was entered on the profile they said a nickname, no street address, no city, no state and no link to their school. But there was one other piece of information on their profile that was giving away where they lived.

Going back to the search engine, let's use the *Friend Finder* search.

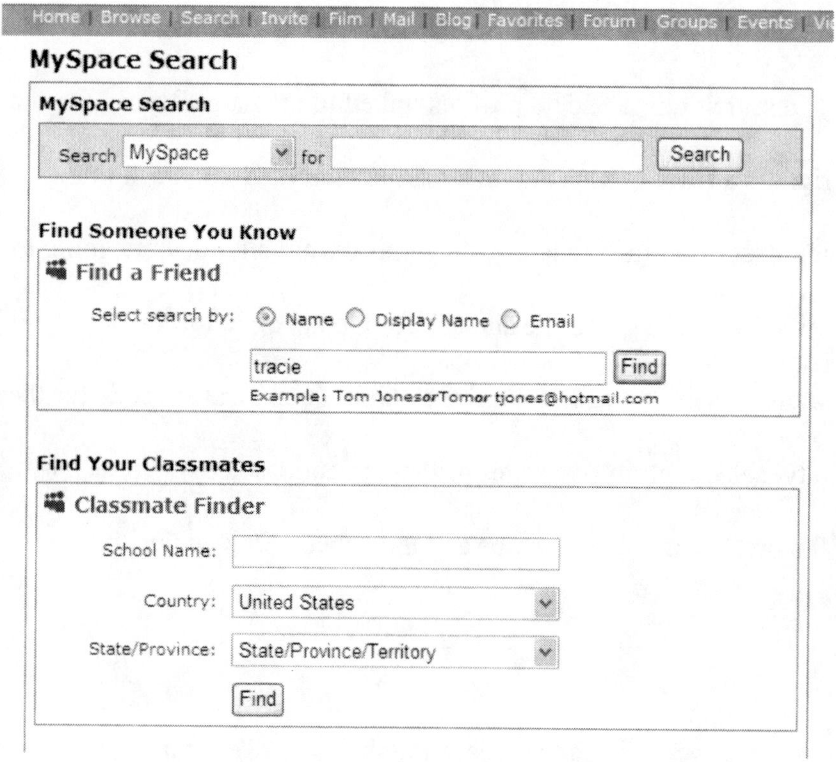

Home | Browse | Search | Invite | Film | Mail | Blog | Favorites | Forum | Groups | Events
MySpace Search
MySpace Search
Search MySpace for
Search
Find Someone You Know
Find a Friend
Select search by: Name Display Name Email
tracie
Find
Example: Tom JonesorTomor tjones@hotmail.com
Find Your Classmates
Classmate Finder
School Name:
Country: United States
State/Province: State/Province/Territory
Find

This search starts with a name, any name. In the example we are looking for a girl named Tracie.

Home | Browse | Search | Invite | Film | Mail | Blog | Favorites | Forum | Groups | Events | Videos | Music | Comedy | Classifieds
Find a Friend
Results for TRACIE
1-10 of 5000
1 2 3 4 5 >> of 500
Next >
Headline:
Orientation:
Here For:
Gender:
Age: 32
Location:
Profile Updated
NO PHOTO
tracie
View Profile
Send Message
Send Instant Message
Forward to a Friend
Add to Blog Preferred List
Filter your Friend Search
located within:
Country: United States
Postal Code: Any miles of 60540
Only show users who have photos
Show name and photos no text
Update

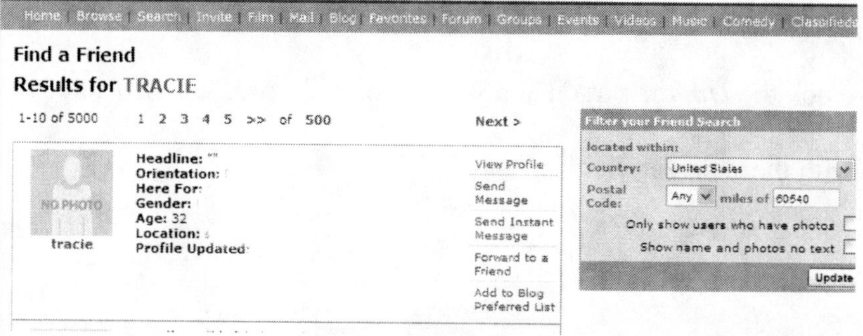

The search revealed 500 profiles linked to the name Tracie. On the right is a filter to assist in refining the search. Going back to the mindset of online predators, they know what city they are going to visit. They can go online and ask for the zip code for the city they want to visit. Using the filter, they would enter the zip code for the city, select within five miles of that zip code, select to view only the profiles that have photos and then check *Show name and photos*.

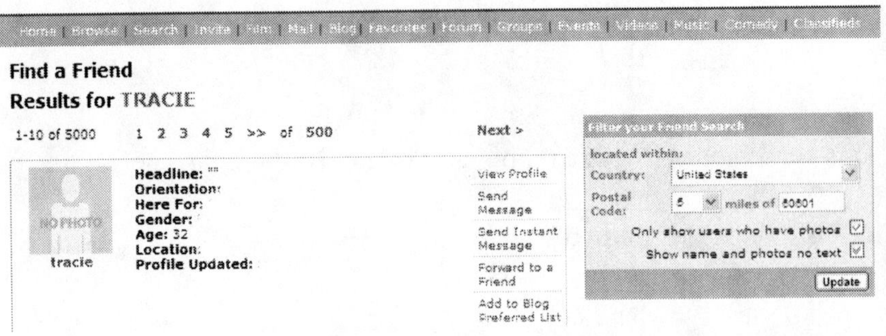

Click the *Update* button and you see only 20 profiles associated with these search fields. .

Included in the 20 profiles is Tracie Smith, who lives in Chicago, Illinois. This is the same profile we created. It took less than a half dozen mouse clicks to go from 220 million users to one specific user.

I would like to see the zip code search field removed from the options. But remember, I look at this as a police officer, and I am sure if MySpace did everything I wanted, they would be out of business in a couple of weeks. That is why working in a cooperative effort with the folks at MySpace is a better way to go than just storming the castle.

III. Viewing My Child's Social Network Profile

So now that you know about MySpace the next logical question is, "How do I see my child's MySpace profile?" I suggest sitting down with your child and asking to see his or her profile. After signing on, you will see the images and videos that have been placed on the profile. Do not be too judgmental about the content. Remember, "Pick your battles." If the information is dangerous to your child, explain why and remove the information. If you just do not like some of the content, but it is not dangerous or illegal, then you might do more harm than good by trying to remove it. Remember, if your children fear punishment they will not confide in you. If you cut them a little slack on some of the content they will be more willing to show you future changes to their MySpace.

Normally, when we are teaching children what is or is not acceptable on a profile we use what we call the "Grandma Rule." If you would not show the content to your Grandmother, then it does not belong online. The fact is, most children do not worry as much about their parents and may actually try to shock them by using outrageous content. But they are usually less willing to shock their Grandma.

After reviewing the images, videos and profile information take a look at their blog. What are they writing about on the blog? Are they putting personal information on their blog? Explain to them that the blog is not private and they may be posting their most personal thoughts to a very public area. This area can include online predators that will use this personal information to initiate contact with them. Online predators can use the personal information to tailor an approach that will allow them to appear to be sympathetic to your child, when in reality they are using this information to begin the grooming process.

After checking the blog, look at who is on their friends list. Take a look at each of the friends and ask your child to explain who they are and how they met that friend. As you go through the list, do not be afraid to click on the friend's link and look over the friend's profile. The image they used in order to be listed on your child's profile may not match all the other images on their profile. The image they used in order to say hello to your child and be listed in the friends section may be a "G" rated image but when you get to the friend's profile the other images are "R" or "X" rated images and videos. Also check the content of the friend's blog. Do you feel it is appropriate content for your child? Did your child post a message on their friend's blog? What rating would you give this content? Your child might keep their profile clean, but post a very different type of content on their friend's blog.

If you are uncomfortable with someone on the friends list tell your child why and ask them to remove that friend. Remind your child that a stranger on the internet should be dealt with in the same manner as a stranger in real life. Stay away from them and tell mom and dad if they persist in trying to make contact with you.

Part of the peer pressure your child faces in regard to having a MySpace profile is, once you have one, you want to yours to be the "coolest." How do you get to be the coolest? The coolest site has the most friends. The way to get the most friends is to accept everyone who asks to join your buddy list. The fact is children will allow hundreds of people to be listed as friends on their profile. Yes, peer pressure exists in cyberspace as well.

Another way to see your child's MySpace profile is to create a MySpace for yourself and use the above search guide to find your child's MySpace. Once you are on your child's profile, look around and decide for yourself if it is safe.

IV. Getting Past the Private Setting

"But I marked my site 'private!' " That statement is probably the one children most often assert during the internet safety presentations. It is probably the excuse we hear most often as to why a child's MySpace is safe. Be careful here, and make sure you understand what "private" actually means.

If your child has marked their site "private," there are several different ways to see the content. One way is to use your MySpace account to send an add request to your child's account. Once you are added, you get to see all the content on the MySpace profile including their list of online friends. This might mean setting up a profile so he or she will not know it is mom and dad asking to join.

When your child creates a MySpace profile he or she has the option to make certain areas of the site private. Different levels of privacy can be selected. Once the profile is created, the access level to different areas of the profile can be changed by clicking on *Account Settings*.

Change Account Settings

NOTE: Changing your default email or name can make it hard for your friends
to find or recognize you on MySpace

[View My Profile] [Edit My Profile] [Cancel Account]

My Account Settings	
Email Address:	tracies123321@yahoo.com
Change Password:	- Change Password: -
Notifications:	☐ Do not send me notification emails -help-
Newsletters:	☐ Do not send me MySpace newsletters
Privacy Settings:	- Change Settings -
IM Privacy Settings:	- Change Settings -
Mobile Settings: New!	- Change Settings -
Groups Settings:	- Change Settings -
Calendar Settings:	- Change Settings -
Blocked Users:	- View List -
Profile Views:	- Reset Count -
Profile Settings:	- Change Settings -
Music Settings: New!	- Change Settings -
Away Message:	- View / Edit Away Message -
Preferred Site & Language:	U.S.A.
Time Zone Settings:	(GMT -08:00 hours) Pacific Time (US & Canada
	-Change-

By using the *Privacy Settings*, you can limit access to your child's MySpace information such as who can see the site and who can send your child an instant message. Select a category and set the appropriate level.

Privacy Settings:

Return to Account Settings

We care about your privacy at MySpace!

To make sure you have a fun and comfortable experience on MySpace, we let you control how other users contact you and view your profile.

- Check to require users to know your email address or last name to send you a friend request.
- Check to review comments to your profile, blog, or photos before they are posted.
- Check to hide your online status from other users.
- Check to alert your friends when your birthday is near.
- Check to prevent other users from emailing links to your photos from the site.
- Check to allow only your friends to post comments on your blog entries.
- Check to block unwanted friend requests from bands.

Who Can View My Full Profile

- ( ) My Friends Only
- (•) Public
- ( ) Only Users Over 18

Privacy Settings

- [ ] Friend Requests - Require email or last name
- [ ] Comments - approve before posting
- [ ] Hide Online Now
- [x] Show My Birthday to my Friends
- [ ] Photos - No Forwarding
- [ ] Blog Comments - Friends Only
- [ ] Friend Requests - No Bands
- [ ] Block Users Under 18 From Contacting Me

Group Invite Privacy Settings

Block Group Invites From:

- [ ] Everyone (including my friends)
- [ ] Users who are not added to my friends
- [x] Bands (who are not added to my friends)
- [x] Filmmakers (who are not added to my friends)
- [x] Comedians (who are not added to my friends)

- Check the box for any group of users that you do not want to recieve Group Invites from. Any box you leave unchecked will allow that set of users to send you Invitations to join a group.

Event Invite Privacy Settings

Block Event Invites From:

- [ ] Everyone (including my friends)
- [ ] Users who are not added to my friends
- [x] Bands (who are not added to my friends)
- [x] Filmmakers (who are not added to my friends)
- [x] Comedians (who are not added to my friends)

- Check the box for any group of users that you do not want to recieve Event Invites from. Any box you leave unchecked will allow that set of users to send you Invitations to attend an event.

[Change Settings] [Cancel]

These settings allow you and your child to select what content and access other MySpace users will have to your child's MySpace profile. Your child can limit who sees his or her profile to only people over 18 or the more restrictive *My Friends Only*. The *My Friends Only* setting means a request must be received from another user to be added to their friends list, and that request must be approved before the other user will have access to your child's information.

Now a word of caution: Do not think that just because your child used the *My Friends Only* setting that online predators will be prevented from getting on the friends list or seeing the content. Due to peer pressure and the desire to be popular and have the "coolest" MySpace profile, most children will add almost anyone who sends them a request to be added.

In addition to adding anyone who sends a request, they almost certainly have already put all the information on their MySpace profile at risk by allowing their best friend to have access. During the internet safety presentations to children we ask them if they marked their site as private. A large majority of the children say they have. We know this is not necessarily accurate because before giving the presentation we searched for the school and found hundreds, if not thousands, of MySpace profiles for the school. In the peer-pressure packed environment of the presentation, some children do not want to be on the outside, so they say they have marked their site as private when in reality they have not. At this point, we ask them whom they added to their MySpace profile and the replies range from "I don't know" to "just my friends." Our next question is, "Did you add your best friend to your MySpace?" Of course the answer is, "Yes." We ask them who is the one person in the world they fight with more than their parents, and often they say their best friend. We point out that they have given access to all their personal information to the one person in the world whom they fight with more than any other person. During one of the times they are fighting with their best friend it would be easy for their best friend to access their MySpace, hit the *Print Screen* button and make a full copy of their site and post it to a new MySpace profile that is not marked private. Anything said on the MySpace profile would now be visible to all other users. As you can see, once your child adds even one person to their "friends" list there is no way to guarantee the information will remain private.

The best way to see your child's MySpace profile is to sit down with him or her and ask to see it. I am not naive enough to believe all children will allow mom and dad to do this. In that case, do as I explained above and create a MySpace profile that you believe your child will allow to be added and send a request to be added.

This method may work for sites you know about, or that your child has allowed you to see, but how do you know if they are just letting you see the MySpace page they know you will approve of and hiding their real MySpace profile from you? This is where filtering programs like Cyber Sentinel can alert you to the existence of the attempt to create other MySpace pages. The attempt to post prohibited information on those pages will alert you to the names of the sites.

In addition to the filters alerting you to the use of prohibited content, the key logging software program, SpectorPro, will alert you to the user name of the MySpace page and the password used to create the site. As I said earlier, I believe telling your child the software is installed on the computer is the way to go. Work with your children, let them know about the software and that it is there to help protect them. The software will work within the rules and guidelines upon which you have agreed. It will act for mom and dad to review content in order to make sure your child is not making a mistake. In time, your child will learn to work with the software and be safer online.

Knowing what your child is doing online can help you keep them safer when they post information, create websites or instant message. But remember, there is no one piece of software or parental control setting that will give you a 100% guarantee to keep your child safe. No software can replace good parenting skills.

One last word of warning about social networking sites, about the content your children post to these sites and the impact it can have on them. Once an image or statement is posted to a blog, your child may lose the ability to delete the content. If someone else saw the site and saved the content, or if an archiving site viewed and saved the site, your child will not be able to delete the content from that other location. In other words, someone or some company made a copy of your child's content and they now control what becomes of that content. This can come back to haunt our children. Say they posted images that seemed funny in college to a social networking site. Five years later they are a kindergarten teacher or might be interviewing for a job and some of the "college images" are found by a parent of one of the kindergarten students or by the interviewer who is doing research on the background of the job candidate. Those images will almost certainly end up in the hands of the principal of the school and ultimately the principal may have to defend the kindergarten teacher, or the job candidate may not be offered the job. Warn you child so that he or she does not end up in this position. Use the Grandma rule: *If Grandma wouldn't approve, do not put it online.*

V. Gateway Social Networking Sites

I am borrowing the term **Gateway Social Networking Sites** from Cara Smith, the Deputy Chief of Staff for the Illinois Attorney General's Office. She coined the phrase and I believe it is a fairly accurate description of these new versions of social networking sites. These gateway sites are the newest form of social networking and are aimed at children between five and 13 years of age. Right now, even your preschooler can have a profile on a social networking site.

The dilemma with these gateway sites is the mixed messages we are sending to our children. On one hand, we tell them in the real world not to talk to strangers. We warn them about putting personal information on profiles or in blogs. They are warned not to tell anyone online their address, birth date or telephone number. This is all still good advice and an easy guideline for children online to follow. When I grew up I heard the same warnings about strangers in the real world. Yet in English class my teacher provided each student with a pen pal in a foreign country and we were encouraged to write to this stranger. The goal was to teach us how to write, use grammar correctly and learn social skills that would help us later in life. Now move forward several decades and that same dynamic is at work, only now it is the internet rather than "snail mail" and it is chatting rather than writing a letter. The fact is the world keeps changing and as any parent can tell you, this constant change is what makes raising a child difficult. Most parents are involved in their child's online habits and just need a little information about the sites so they can make an educated decision about what sites their children should be using.

Two of the more popular gateway social networking sites are Club Penguin and Webkinz. In a moment I will take you inside these two sites and explain how they work and how they may be a safer place for younger children. Keep in mind you are not alone, you are not the only one confronted with having your child online at a younger and younger age. The fact is this generation of children is going to grow up in a world where there has always been an internet. Computers, chat, profiles and social networking via the internet will be a normal part of their everyday life. To make sure they are using all of these in the safest possible manner parents need a basic understanding of how the sites function.

Do not be afraid that your children are online and in these gateway social networking sites at a younger age. It can give parents the early opportunity to start teaching their children how to be safer online. As you will learn, the way Club Penguin and Webkinz have used menu driven chat and limited vocabularies, their sites provide a safer online experience for children.

One of the most popular of these new gateway social networking sites is Club Penguin. The designers of the site have taken the concept of children's online safety seriously and have incorporated that mindset throughout their site. Both Club Penquin and Webkinz have two types of chats. One is menu driven in that the children do not actually type the content of chat messages. Instead, the messages are selected from predetermined phrases. In Club Penguin this is called Ultimate Safe Chat and in Webkinz it is called Kinz Chat. Both sites also have chat where your children can type in the content of the chat. It is called Standard Safe Chat on Club Penguin and on Webkinz it is called Kinz Chat Plus. I am using some of the screen shots from Club Penguin to illustrate how the different chats are chosen and how they work.

Let's look at the Ultimate Safe Chat first. In this version your child does not have the ability to type in chat. Instead they must select what to say from a list of predetermined phrases.

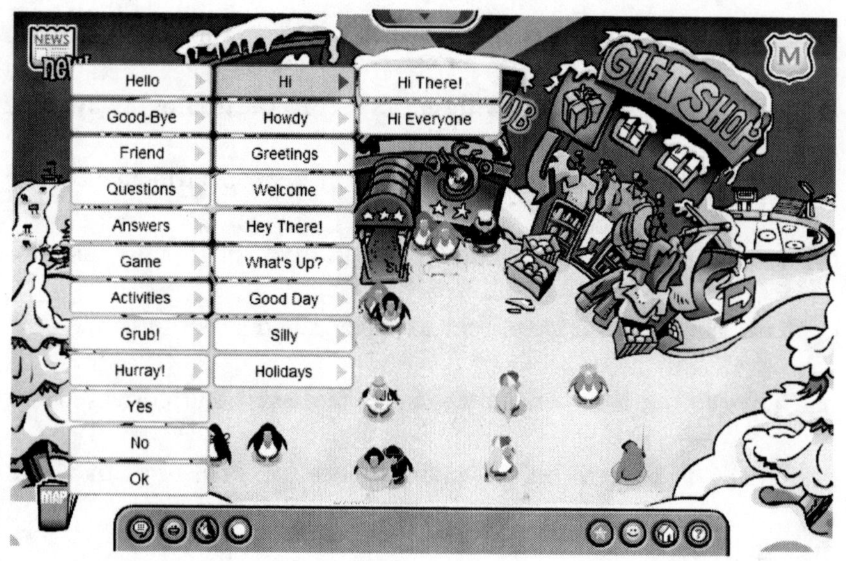

In this example we wanted to say, "Hello" and the options were; "Hi," "Hi There!" or "Hi Everyone." We could drop down one menu and see the sayings for "Howdy" or "Greetings" and so on. If you look at the bottom of the screen you notice that the blue rectangle is covering the chat box that would normally be seen.

It is not so much the content of the greeting, but the format that makes this chat safer. In this format it is not possible to ask questions such as, "What is your name?" "Where do you live?" "What is your phone number?" or "Would you like to meet in real life?" Since those types of predatory questions do not appear as options in the menus it is not possible to ask them. They can chat to people they just met without the fear of giving away any personal information, being spoken to in disrespectful manner or being confronted with sexually suggestive or openly hostile content. This has the same feel as when I had to write to my pen pal. I wrote the letter and my teacher reviewed and corrected the grammar and content before I could write the final draft that was eventually sent.

One thing to note here is that I have removed the screen names of all the penguins. Normally each penguin's screen name would appear next to the penguin; however, to protect the privacy of each penguin I have masked all the screen names.

The second manner of chatting on Club Penguin and Webkinz allows your child to enter the content of the chat by typing what they want to say. However, whatever they type will be checked and if it matches the "allowed" content it will be posted to the room. If it does not match, no other child in the chat room will see the content. The two sites use different methods to decide what is allowed chat. In Webkinz they created their own dictionary of words. If the word appears in the dictionary created by Webkinz then the content is allowed to be seen in the chat room. If the content does not appear in their dictionary it cannot be seen.

Club Penguin uses the filter method of choosing what content can or cannot be seen. Their filters look for harmful words and sexually oriented or openly hostile content and they do not allow such content to be displayed. As you can imagine, this form of filtering needs constant updating. When we tried to get around the filter in tests of different phrases or predatory phrases we were blocked. In one instance, we were actually banned from the site for 24 hours for using inappropriate language. These bans can be 24 hours, 72 hours or expulsion from the site.

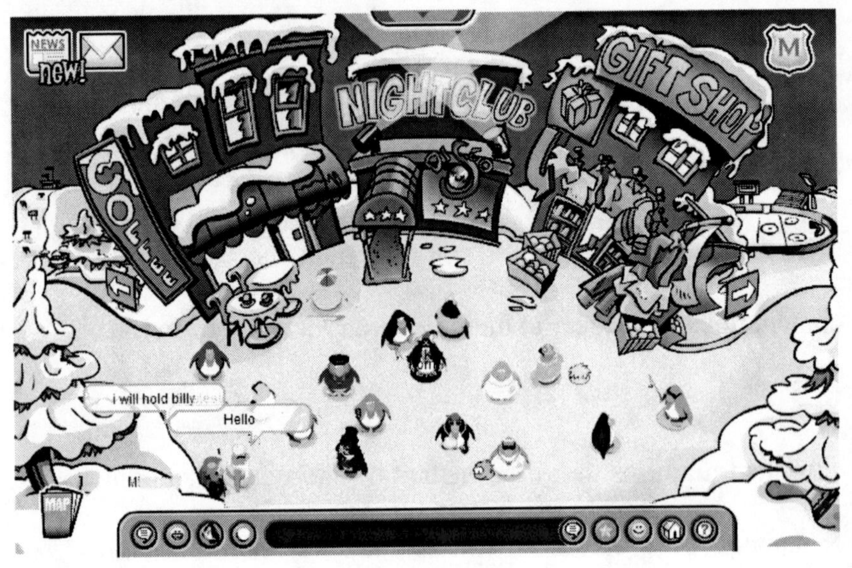

In the Standard Safe Chat version the dark blue rectangle at the bottom of the screen is where the chat is typed. Once the chat phrase has been typed, it is sent and the filter reviews it for content and for the version of the chat being used. If you are using Standard Chat but your friend is using Ultimate they will not be able to see anything you type. Remember Ultimate Chat is menu driven so it will not allow anyone to use the Standard Chat format to interact with your child. If both children are using the Standard Chat format the content is checked by the filter and if it is allowed content the other child will be able to see what it says.

We wondered about using codes to try and sneak through some personal information.

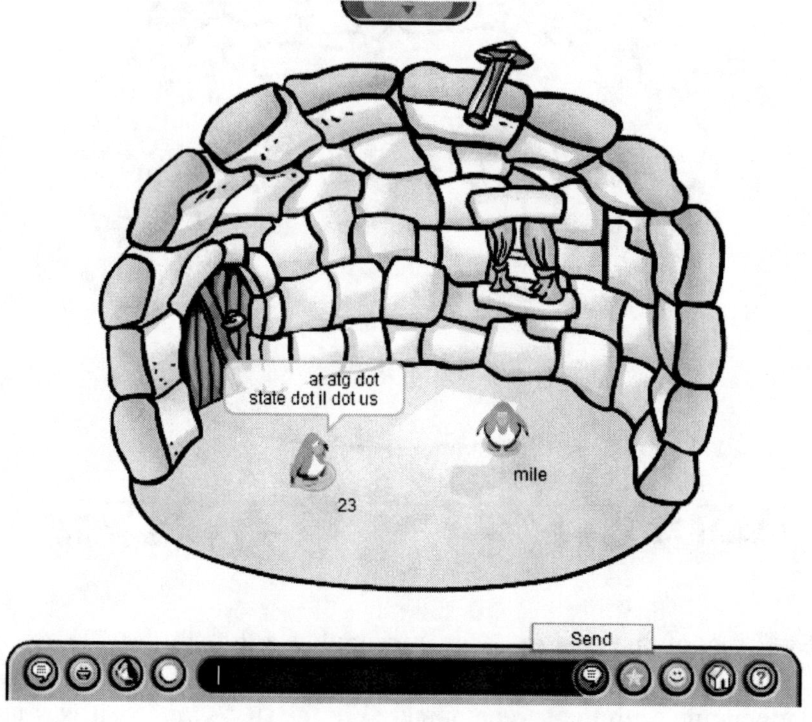

In this example we tried to sneak an email address past the filter. We are the penguin with the screen name 23. We sent the chat to the penguin using the screen name mile. We used the word “dot” for the period in the address and the word “at” for the @ sign. This also was also a test between Standard Safe Chat and Ultimate Safe Chat.

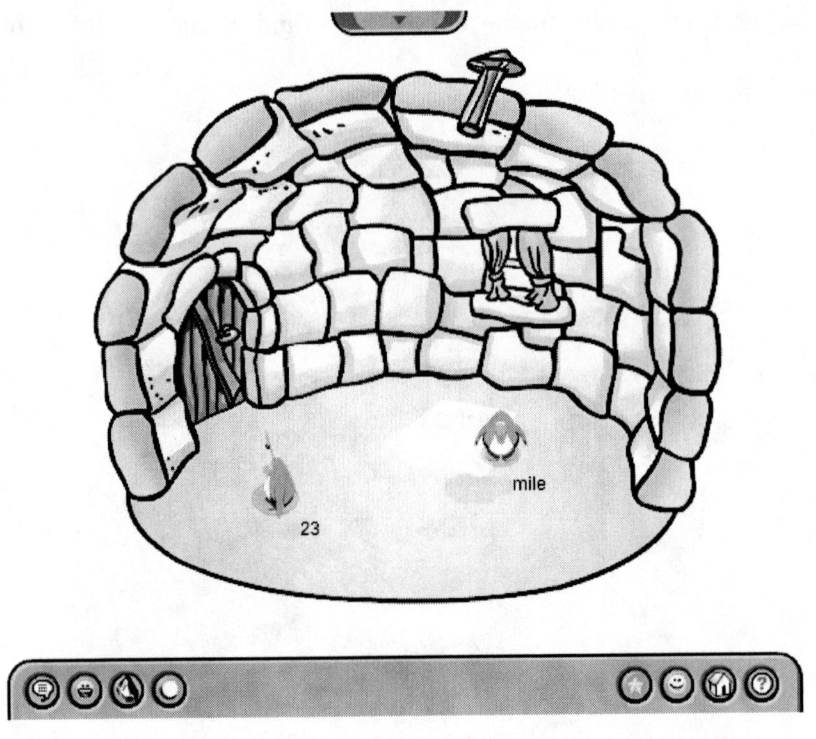

Even though the chat message appeared as a thought bubble above the penguin with the screen name 23 in the first graphic, it was not displayed on the screen of the penguin who was using the screen name mile. The filter removed the content but did not inform the sender that the message was not received. This method is used to prevent Safe Chat and Ultimate Safe Chat users from exchanging any non-menu driven content. Also if it had been two Safe Chat users the filter would have blocked the exchange because the word "at" and the word "dot" were being used to send an email address. The exchange of personal information such as email addresses is not allowed.

When we tried to be more aggressive and sent the word "rape" we received a notice of what word was used and that it triggered a ban.

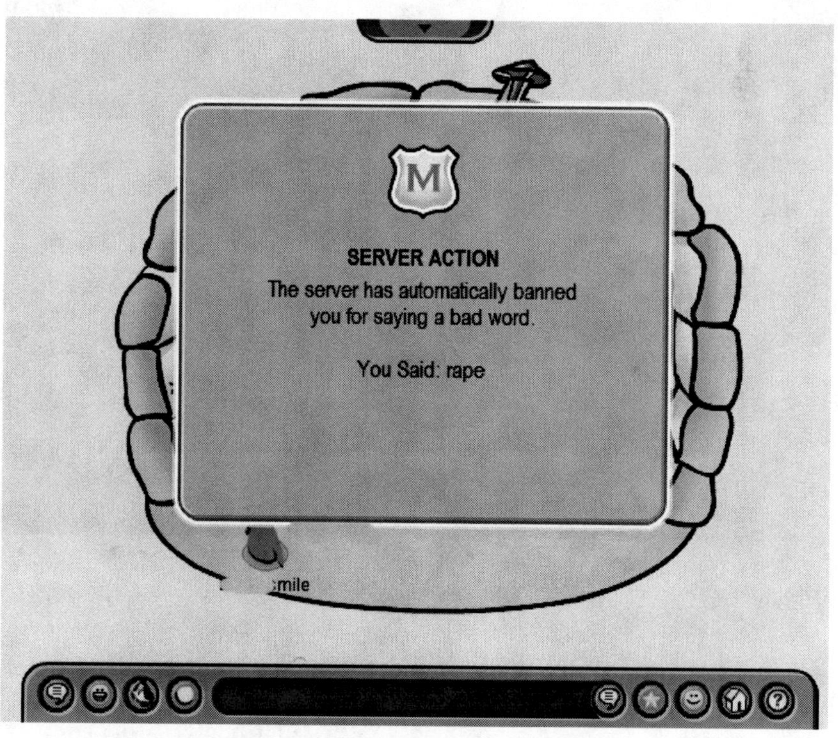

After receiving the notification of the ban for saying an inappropriate word we were notified as to the time frame of the ban.

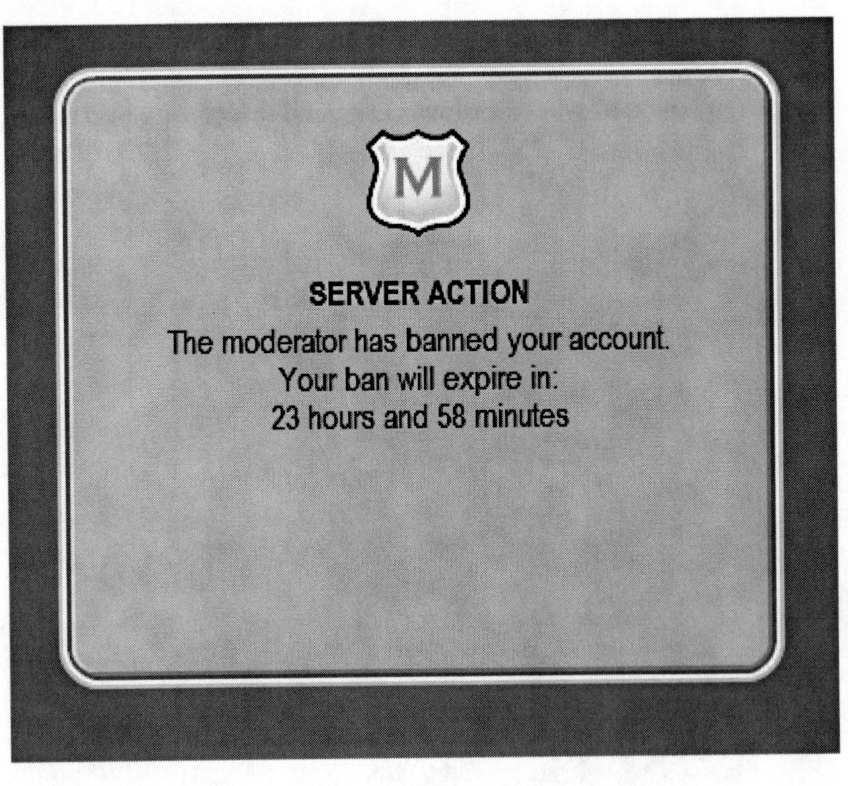

We tried several other tests of the filter. We tried spelling out a phone number, such as (630) 555-1234, which became "six, three, zero, five, five, five, one, two, three, four." The filter blocked that content. We were unsuccessful during several attempts to use shorthand language or children's codes to get personal information through on the Standard Safe Chat. As you can see, this filter does require constant updating to stay current as children change the type of chat shorthand and secret codes. In combination with a live person acting as a moderator for the room and the filters looking for prohibited content, Club Penguin has created a safer environment for children. As it exists, it would be very difficult for a sexual predator to use this form of online communication to lure a child from their home. Does this mean that online predators will not be using Webkinz or Club Penguin? I do not think anyone can say definitively that online predators will not try this format. However, since there are so many unprotected children on other formats I personally do not think online predators will see sites like Club Penguin or Webkinz as a preferred method of interacting with children.

Keep in mind that both of the sites do have a monetary cost. For Club Penguin there is a monthly fee to belong to the site. Once you join the site it is incumbent upon you to opt out and stop the automatic monthly charge to your credit card. With Webkinz you purchase stuffed animals and then go online and enter the secret code on the stuffed animal to adopt the animal. There is no limit to the number of animals one child can adopt. As children make mistakes and are banned or expelled from these sites, they will want to open another account under a different name so they can keep up with their friends on the sites. As parents you can see how the use of inappropriate language and being banned can get costly. This is another reason to be involved in teaching your child appropriate online conduct.

VI. Online Dating

Children are not the only ones who need to be careful about using social networking sites. Many adults meet people online with the hope of eventually meeting them in person for dating or relationships. Registered sex offenders use the computer, the internet, social networking sites and now online dating sites to find their next victims.

How is this occurring? Sexual predators sign onto a dating site and tailor their information so they will meet people who have children. They specifically indicate they are looking for other people who have children and may even specify the age of the children. The age specified is the age of the children the online predator prefers to molest. I know this sounds insidious, however it does occur.

Online dating sites now have to deal with registered sex offenders and online predators who try to use their service as a hunting ground. Not all registered sex offenders are necessarily online predators, however I think most people entering into a new relationship would like to know if the person they are meeting is a registered sex offender.

Social networking sites have begun using software that allows their sites to be checked against the list of registered sex offenders. Because of these checks, a large number of registered sex offenders and some very dangerous online predators have been removed from these social networking sites. These registries are public information. I will show you where to find some of the registries online at the end of this chapter.

With only some basic information, it is simple to find out if someone is listed as a registered sex offender. The easiest way is to search by the person's name. The problem here is being sure you have their real name. When the social networking sites began searching for registered sex offenders they searched by name. One site found over 29,000 profiles that related to registered sex offenders using their real names. This does not account for the ones who lied or changed their name.

Most of the sex offender registries allow for the offenders to be searched through a variety of data fields. The searches can be conducted by name, address, city, county, state or zip code. Knowing the data fields can help you to discover if the person you are thinking of meeting is registered.

Some simple guidelines for adults who are considering meeting someone they met online in real life:

- Meet in a public place. Make it a place you are comfortable with, but not necessarily close to where you live. This way the other person will not know your address or even your neighborhood. If you get a bad feeling during the meeting you can simply walk away without any concern that the other person will show up at your work or home.
- Bring a friend with you to the first meeting. When we were all little and on a school field trip or scouting trip, we were taught to use the buddy rule. No one could go anywhere alone, you had to have your buddy with you at all times. What I suggest is to tell the person you intend to meet that you will be bringing a friend. If your new online friend balks at your bringing a friend to the meeting or you arrive at the meeting spot and your online friend does not show up it should be a red flag. This may indicate your new

online friend does not want a witness to your meeting. He will have an excuse when you sign back online or exchange emails and ask to meet again. If he gives you any trouble about bringing a friend do not meet him. Another method is to just take a friend with you and not tell your online friend you are bringing someone. He may have actually gone to the meeting location, but when he sees you brought a witness and he will leave. He will have an excuse for not making the meeting and ask to meet again. This time tell him you are bringing a friend and if he questions why you need a friend you will know this is a major red flag.

- Ask the person for his address or city and suggest you will pick him up and bring him to the meeting location. Then later call him and tell him an unforeseen incident has kept you longer and you will meet him at the public place. I know this will sound sexist, but in my experience, the vast majority of sexual offenders and online predators are male. I have been involved in and heard of others arresting female sexual predators. However, the overwhelming majority of these predators have been male. Keeping that in mind, I suggest women ask to pick up their date so they can learn the geographical area where their date lives. The geographical information can be used to search the registries. Even if the predator lied about his name, the registries can be searched by address, city, state or zip code. Most of the registries include a recent photograph of the registered sex offender. You can compare the picture online in the registry to the image used on the dating site.

- Do not give out your address or home telephone number when setting up your first meeting. Avoid giving out your work telephone number because a search online of the telephone number may show your work address. I know this may conflict with the tip above, but if possible use a cell phone, although do so with the understanding that even some cell phones can be searched online for an address associated with the it. I suggest anyone with children who is using an online dating site ask for the other person's address and telephone number but guard your own. I know this may seem harsh to some, but bearing the embarrassment of asking and checking the registries will far outweigh the feeling of guilt if something should happen to your child. If the person you are meeting truly is a good person they will probably appreciate meeting someone with the common sense to be safe when meeting strangers.

- Check the online dating site's policies and procedures to see what safeguards they have in place to prevent online predators from using their site. Keep in mind policies and procedures cannot prevent every online predator from gaining entry to these sites. Use their policies and procedures as the first line of defense and your common sense and checking the registries as a second and third line of defense.

How do you find the online sex offender registries for your area? The easiest way is to use a search engine like Google.

Type in "sex offender registry."

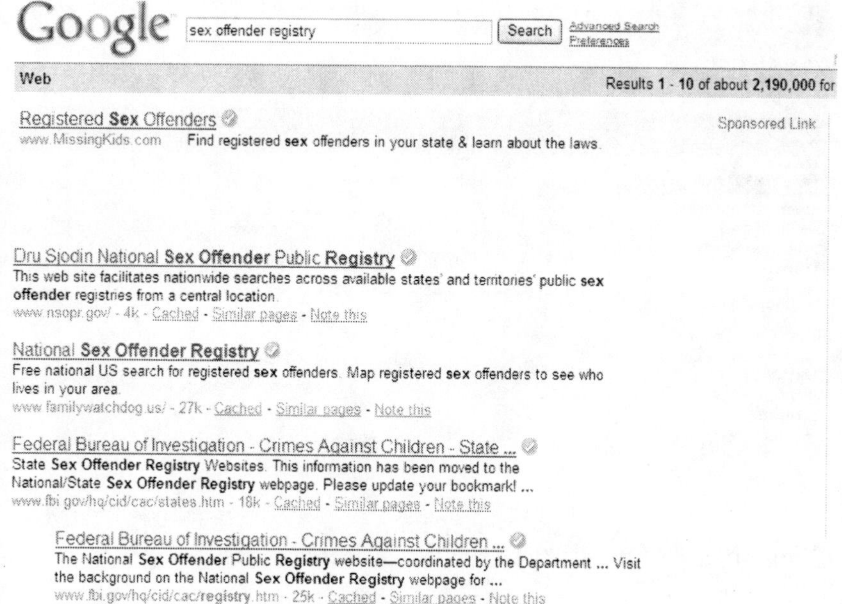

This provides a link to several good sites to check the online sex offender registries for the nation.

The first site www.missingkids.com will take you to the National Center for Missing and Exploited Children.

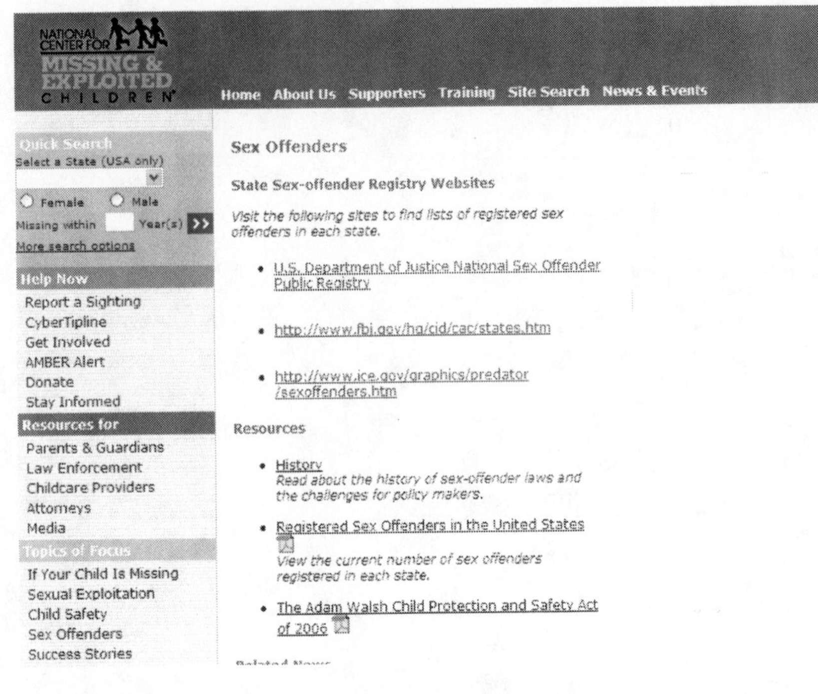

Click on any of the links to see the different registries.

The second link listed on our Google search was www.nsopr.gov. Clicking on that link brings us to the Dru Sjodin National Sex Offender Registry.

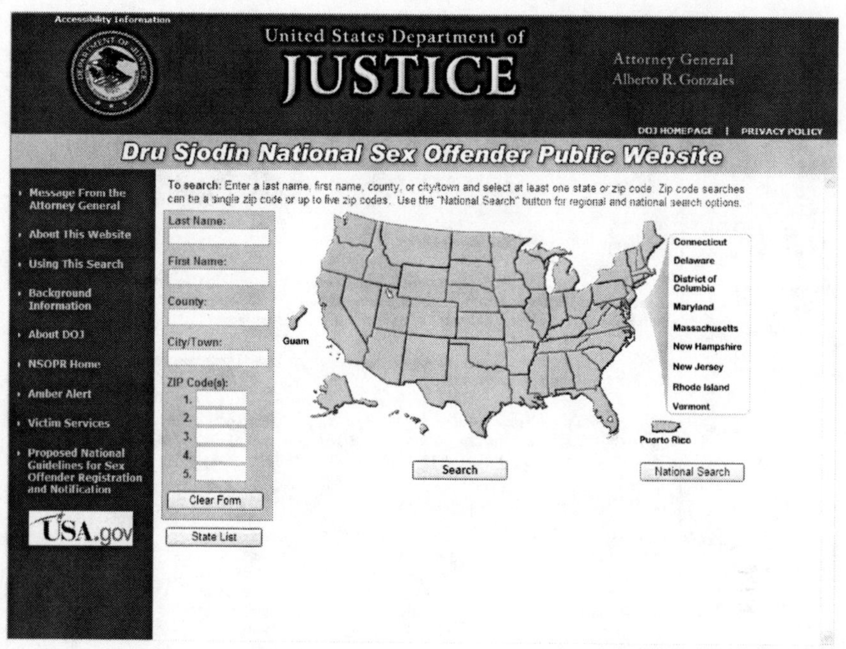

This site allows you to search multiple zip codes at one time.

One of the other sites you can use is

http://www.fbi.gov/hq/cid/cac/registry.htm.

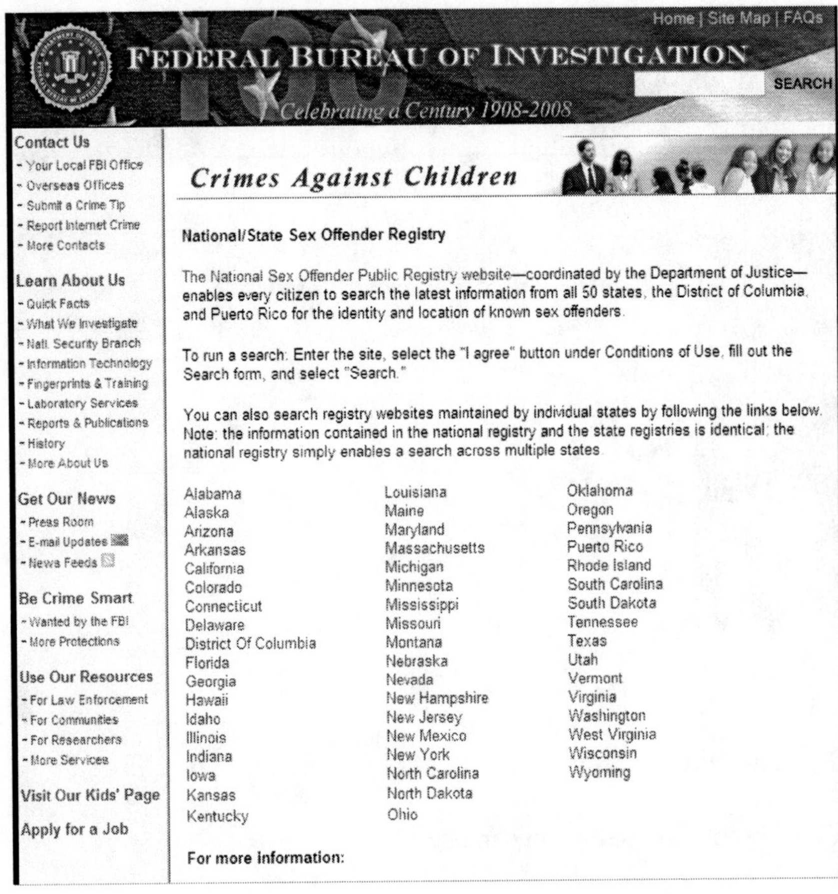

This site allows you to select the state first and then move on to name, address and zip code. Above I selected the state of Illinois. The link took me to the sex offender registry for the state of Illinois maintained by the Illinois State Police. If the links above do not work, try finding the state police website for your home state. Many of the sex offender registries are maintained by the state police.

The link for the Illinois Sex Offender Registry is http://www.isp.state.il.us/sor. After clicking on the *Terms of Use Agreement* you will see the Illinois Sex Offender registry.

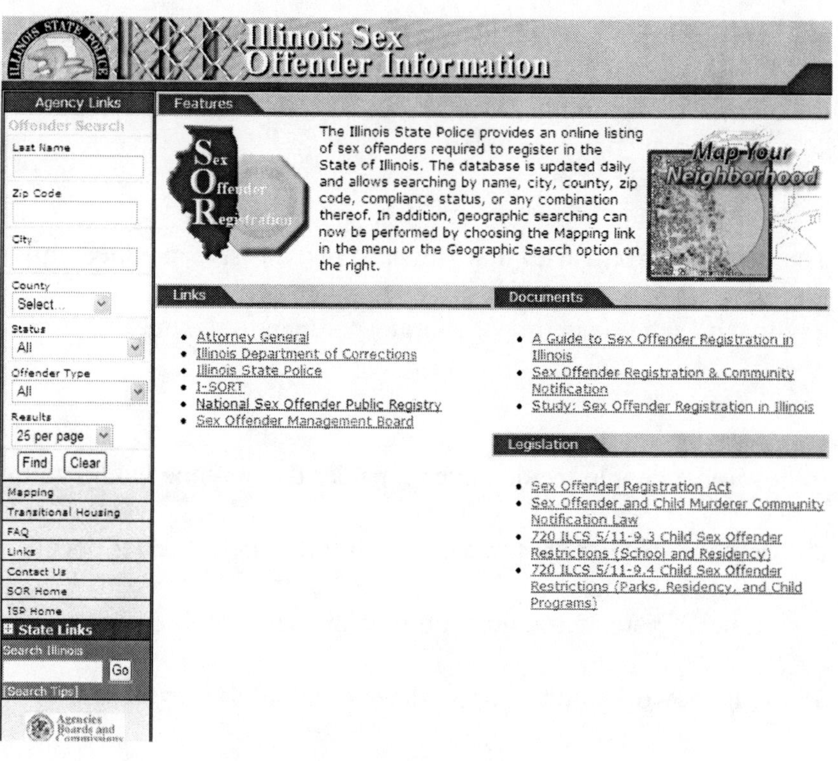

On the upper left you see the different search data fields that can be used. You only need to put information in one of the fields to receive results for your search. Obviously, the more information you have the more successful your search. If you only have the zip, the results of your search will show every registered sex offender for that zip and you will have to search each picture to see if it matches the online profile. If you have the last name your search may only return a few results and it will be easier to find a picture to compare to the online profile.

There are other registries that you can check. I have supplied only a few, but each one is free of charge and open to the public.

I know most people would never consider that anyone would go to this depth of deceit to get to a child. Unfortunately, it does occur sometimes. There are no guarantees when using online sites, so do a little homework and try to use the sites as safely as you can.

CHAPTER 5:
WHERE CAN I TURN FOR HELP?

The following is a list of websites with content to help parents and children understand the online world. The list is in alphabetical order, so the order in which a site is listed does not represent its value. This list is not meant to be all inclusive. The sites' various types of content include tips for parents, tips for children, full curriculums for teachers and school districts and contact numbers for computer-literate police officers.

I. Illinois Attorney General's Website

The Illinois Attorney General's office website has many helpful tips for parents and children. The site has a specific location to find online contracts for parents, children and teachers. When you sit down to discuss what proper online behavior is, these contracts can be very useful. I recommend reading them with your child. After reading them, both of you should sign them and then tape it to the side of your monitor for future reference.

To find the contracts go to http://www.illinoisattorneygeneral.gov.

Click on *Safeguarding Children.*

ILLINOIS ATTORNEY GENERAL Lisa Madigan

www.IllinoisAttorneyGeneral.gov

Home | Press Room | Legislation | Opinions | Español | Other Languages | Photos | Site Map | Contact Us

About Us
Protecting Consumers
Advocating for Women
Keeping Communities Safe
Advocating for Older Citizens
Safeguarding Children
Defending Your Rights
Preserving the Environment
Helping Crime Victims
Ensuring Open and Honest Government
Building Better Charities
MethNet

Acrobat® Reader® software is needed to view and print PDF documents available from this website.

Safeguarding Children

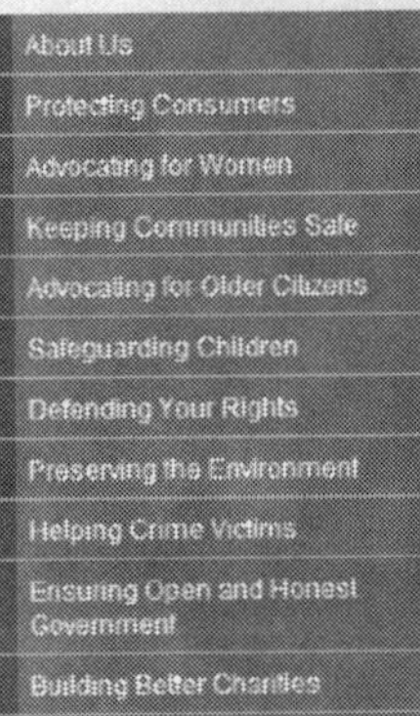

The Office of the Attorney General is committed to making sure our children are able to grow up in a safe community. As part of this commitment, we have established the Youth Advocacy Initiative, a project that focuses on juvenile justice and youth advocacy. In addition, we are working on a number of programs designed to keep kids safe including "Surf Safe: Navigating the Hidden Dangers of the Internet," and a teen dating violence education campaign.

Many of the programs listed on this page are part of the Attorney General's Youth Advocacy Initiative, a project that focuses on juvenile justice and youth advocacy. You may also find additional information about the Youth Advocacy Initiative and other programs related to community safety on our Keeping Communities Safe page. In the future, look for a link here to our Kids' Page containing activities and information for kids of all ages.

Please follow the links below to find out more information about the Attorney General's initiatives to safeguard children.

Child Support Awareness
Illinois Youth Court Association
Internet Safety
School Violence Tip Line
Teen Dating Violence
Crime Victim Services
Information on Sex Offenders
Childhood Lead Poisoning Prevention
Safe Kids: Protecting Children from Unintentional Injury
Protecting Children from Unsafe Children's Products

Return to Home Page

© 2007 Illinois Attorney General

Home • Privacy Policy • Contact Us

Click on *Internet Safety*.

ILLINOIS ATTORNEY GENERAL Lisa Madigan

www.IllinoisAttorneyGeneral.gov

Home | Press Room | Legislation | Opinions | Español | Other Languages | Photos | Site Map | Contact Us

Safeguarding Children

- About Us
- Protecting Consumers
- Advocating for Women
- Keeping Communities Safe
- Advocating for Older Citizens
- Safeguarding Children
- Defending Your Rights
- Preserving the Environment
- Helping Crime Victims
- Ensuring Open and Honest Government
- Building Better Charities
- MethNet

Internet Safety

The Internet and e-mail have become one of the most common ways for people to communicate with each other. Many people conduct business, shop, research and do a host of other activities online.

However, the anonymous environment of the Internet can be dangerous. The reality of the Internet is that we never really know if the people we are talking to are really who they say they are.

To give parents the tools needed to keep their kids safe on the Internet, Attorney General Madigan has created an innovative program regarding the realities of online safety. This program, Project Surf Safe: Navigating the Hidden Dangers of the Internet, is a useful tool in helping parents stay informed about the dangers lurking on the Internet.

In addition, the Attorney General's office provides online safety tips for children, teenagers and parents as well as other consumer-related information on protecting yourself online.

All of the above information has been designed to help you protect your family when surfing the Internet. However, you are not alone in this fight. The Attorney General's High Tech Crimes Bureau and the Illinois Internet Child Exploitation Task Force are dedicated to stopping online child exploitation.

Please follow the links below to learn more about protecting your family online.

Project Surf Safe Fact Sheet

Online Safety Tips

High Tech Crimes Bureau/Illinois Child Exploitation Task Force

For more information on High Tech Crimes and Internet Safety, please visit the Keeping Communities Safe page on the Attorney General's Web site.

Return to Safeguarding Children

Return to Home Page

© 2007 Illinois Attorney General

Home • Privacy Policy • Contact Us

Click on *Online Safety Tips*.

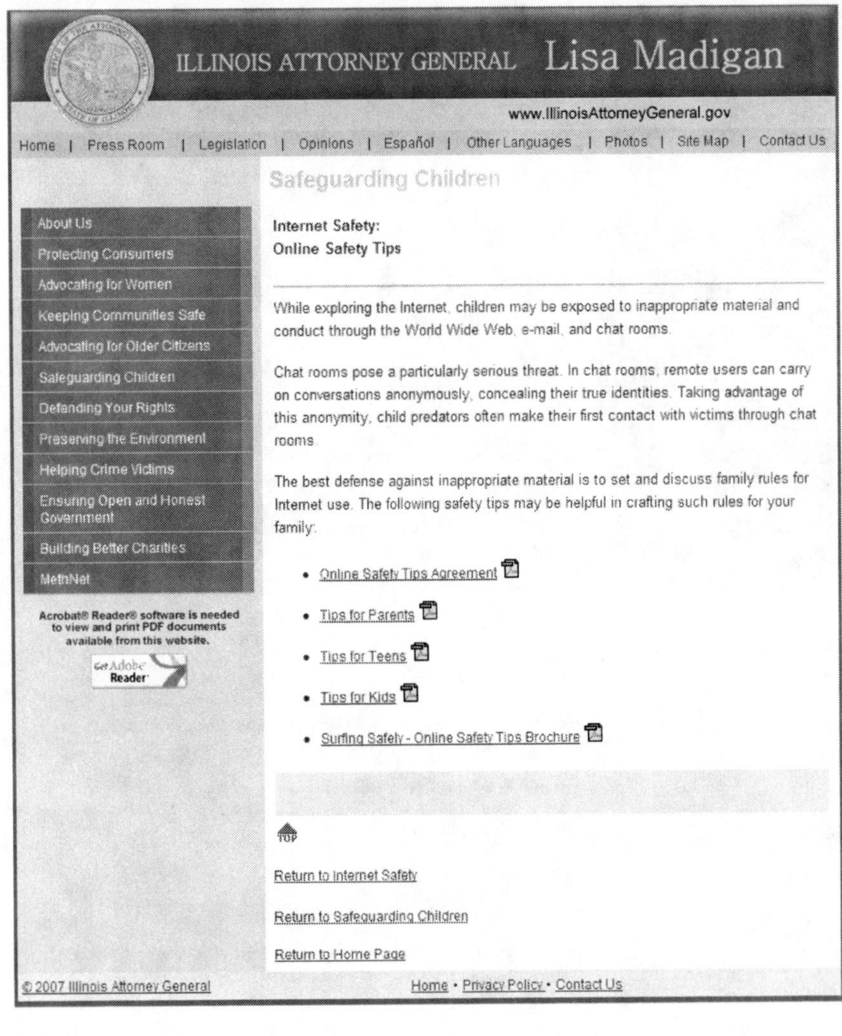

The first document listed is the Agreement. Print this document out and read it with your child. As I suggested above, after you both sign it, post it somewhere in a prominent location by the computer.

That way, when your child tries to use the excuse, "I didn't know," you have the rules in writing right in front of them.

AGREEMENT
TO ABIDE BY THE RULES

PARENTS: PLEASE DISCUSS THIS AGREEMENT WITH YOUR CHILDREN, SIGN IT TOGETHER AND POST IT NEAR YOUR COMPUTER.

I WILL not give out personal information such as my address, telephone number, parents' work addresses/telephone numbers, or the name of my school without my parents' permission.

I WILL tell my parents right away if I come across information that makes me feel uncomfortable.

I WILL never agree to get together with someone I "meet" online without first checking with my parents. If my parents agree to the meeting, I will be sure that it is in a public place and bring my mother or father along.

I WILL never send a person my picture or anything else without first checking with my parents.

I WILL not respond to any messages that are mean or in any way make me feel uncomfortable. It is not my fault if I get a message like that. If I do, I will tell my parents right away so they can contact the Internet service provider.

I WILL talk with my parents so that we can set up rules for going online. We will decide upon the time of day that I can be online, the length of time I can be online, and appropriate areas for me to visit. I will not access other areas or break these rules without their permission.

______________________ ______________________

CHILD **PARENT(S)**

Illinois Attorney General Lisa Madigan • Illinois PTA

Report Internet child exploitation to www.IllinoisAttorneyGeneral.gov

These rules are excerpted and reprinted from *Child Safety on the Information Superhighway* by Lawrence J. Magid. They are reprinted with permission of the National Center for Missing and Exploited Children (NCMEC).

This document is free and can be distributed to any of your neighbors, friends or your children's classmates.

Another site offered by the Illinois Attorney General's office is the Illinois Internet Crimes Against Children's Task Force website. This can be found at http://illinoisicac.org. The site offers many useful tools. The banner at the top is a live feed courtesy of the National Center for Missing and Exploited Children. The feed contains images of children missing from the state of Illinois.

Home | Internet 101 | News & Events | Resources | Contact Us | Privacy Policy

ILLINOIS' MISSING CHILDREN

Have you seen these missing child?

Call 1-800-THE-LOST

A message from the Attorney General

As the Attorney General for the state of Illinois I have always been committed to the protection and safety of the citizens of Illinois. As a parent I also recognize the added challenge of protecting our children from the online attacks of sexual predators using the Internet. On this site you will find answers to some of the most often asked questions about the online world. There are also links and an email address to assist you in reporting criminal acts such as child pornography, sexual solicitation of a child, and how to report a missing child.

Lisa Madigan

Illinois Attorney General web site

CHILD EXPLOITATION
TASK FORCE

www.illinoisicac.org

While exploring the Internet, children may be exposed to inappropriate material and conduct through the World Wide Web, e-mail, and chat rooms. Chat rooms pose a particularly serious threat. In chat rooms, remote users can carry on conversations anonymously, concealing their true identities. Taking advantage of this anonymity, child predators often make their first contact with victims through chat rooms and instant messages. The best defense against inappropriate material is to set and discuss family rules for Internet use. The following safety tips may be helpful in crafting such rules for your family:

http://www.illinoisattorneygeneral.gov/children/safetytips.html

To report online child exploitation, send an e-mail to:
illinoisicactip@atg.state.il.us.

To make an anonymous report click or call the CYBER TIPLINE

INTERNET 101
What is...

- The Internet
- A chat room
- An instant message
- An email message
- A website
- A file
- A jpg, gif, mpg, mp3
- A trojan
- Spyware
- A blog or online journal
- A profile

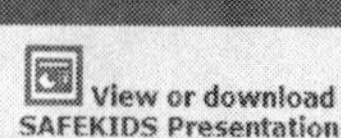

XML

Illinois Missing Children Alerts RSS Feed

What are RSS Feeds?

Home | Internet 101 | News & Events | Resources | Contact Us | Privacy Policy

On the top right is an *Internet 101* for parents. Want to find out what any of those terms mean? Click on the term and a definition will appear.

Just below the *Internet 101* section is a link to the *Safekids* presentation. Safekids is a free PowerPoint presentation on internet safety. The presentation is geared to children in the third or fourth grade. The presentation is fully narrated with nationally known newscasters donating their voices to the presentation. Both the presentation and workbook are available free of cost and Microsoft included a free viewer so you do not need to buy Microsoft PowerPoint. Each slide has notes informing the presenter what concept the slide is trying to convey to the children.

The SOR link connects to the Illinois Sex Offender Registry. This registry allows people in Illinois to search for registered sex offenders by name, city, county or zip code. Many other states have similar registries.

The link directly below the SOR icon takes the viewer to the website for the National Center for Missing and Exploited Children (NCMEC). This link and the links built into the AMBER Alert and CyberTipline all take the viewer to pages within the website for NCMEC. We will look at what these links do a little later in this chapter when we visit the National Center for Missing and Exploited Children's website.

The last link on the page is the ICAC (Internet Crimes Against Children Task Force) and we will look at their website next.

II. The Internet Crimes Against Children Task Force

The Internet Crimes Against Children Task Force (ICAC) is funded by grants from the Department of Justice (DOJ) and the Office of Juvenile Justice and Delinquency Prevention (OJJDP). Currently there are 46 funded and operating franchises of these task forces across the United States. There are additional sites being considered for new members to the task force. To find the nearest task force to your home, visit http://icactraining.org.

Hover over the blue dot in your state and it will display the contact information for the Task Force contact person in your area.

For Illinois, there are two such contacts and the one displayed below is the contact from the Illinois Attorney General's Office.

Illinois

Illinois Attorney General's Office
Jurisdiction: Illinois
Contact: Bureau Chief David Haslett
Phone: (312) 814-6121
E-mail: dhaslett@atg.state.il.us

This site is important to law enforcement officials, as it lists the training available via the ICAC Grants, OJJDP and Fox Valley Technical College which serves as the training arm of the task force. Click on the *Training* tab at the top of the page to see a list of trainings available.

- ICAC-IT
- ICAC-CSO
- ICAC-UC
- ICAC-TAP
- ICAC-US
- CyberTips
- Peer Precision
- National Conf
- SVICAC Conf
- Other

Training

The ICAC Training and Technical Assistance Program is funded through the Office of Juvenile Justice and Delinquency Prevention and provides training in cooperation with Fox Valley Technical College to state and local law enforcement agencies affiliated with OJJDP's Regional ICAC Task Force.

ICAC Training & TA Program Course Offerings

You must obtain authorization from your regional ICAC Task Force prior to submitting a registration form for these training programs.

- ICAC Investigative Techniques Training Program (ICAC-IT)

  The purpose of this 4-1/2 day training program is to provide state and local law enforcement investigators with a basic understanding of investigative techniques in the area of Internet crimes against children. These techniques have been developed by the ICAC Task Force and conform to a set of national standards. Max class size: 30

- ICAC Child Sex Offender Accountability Training Program (ICAC-CSO)

  This newly developed course of instruction is a 4-1/2 day technology training program for law enforcement investigators, probation/parole officers and prosecutors responsible for monitoring or investigating the activities of convicted child sex offenders. Max class size: 30

- ICAC Undercover Chat Investigations Training Program (ICAC-UC)

  An intensive 4-1/2 day training program for experienced ICAC investigators designed to provide them with the latest tools and techniques necessary to combat on-line child exploitation. Max class size: 30

- ICAC Trial Advocacy for Prosecutors Training Program (ICAC-TAP)

  This 4-1/2 day training program is a trial advocacy course involving computer-facilitated crimes against children. It is for experienced prosecutors and is focused on examining the distinct phases of a trial and the relevant issues, challenges, tactics, strategies, and the law that enhance the skills and knowledge of prosecutors in these cases. This course presents significant training on the authentication of technical evidence; how to prepare and organize your case, the selection of jurors, motions practice in computer cases involving crimes against children, the presentation of expert and fact testimony, cross-examination of defendants and their experts as well as how to conduct effective opening statements and closing arguments, among other topics in trial advocacy in such cases. Post-verdict motions and sentencing issues are discussed and analyzed in this course. It is highly recommended that students attend PCO-PRO I before applying to attend this course. This course is heavily influenced by the investigative protocols and standards of the Department of Justice, Office of Juvenile Justice and Delinquency Prevention, Internet Crimes Against Children Task Force. Max class size: 30

- ICAC Unit Supervisor Training Program (ICAC-US)

  This course is currently under development. It will be a 4-1/2 day course for ICAC unit commanders and supervisors for ICAC Task Force and affiliated law enforcement agencies. This training program provides students with an overview of managerial, investigative and early intervention strategies to more effectively protect children in their area of responsibility. Experts in the field of Internet exploitation will review emerging technologies and update participants on current investigative and prosecutorial issues associated with supervising an ICAC unit. Max class size: 48

- CyberTips Management Training Program

  This 2-1/2 day class imparts the skills necessary to use the CyberTips software application developed for use with the NCMEC VPN. It has been designed to enhance the use of the NCMEC CyberTipline Program. Max class size: 24

- Peer Precision Training Program

  This 3-1/2 day class imparts the skills necessary to investigate the use of the peer-to-peer file sharing networks using advanced technology developed as a result of previous peer-to-peer investigations. Max class size: 20

- 2007 Annual ICAC National Conference, San Jose, CA (October 15-19, 2007)

  Each year, the ICAC National Conference is designed to bring hundreds of federal, state and local law enforcement investigators, forensic experts and prosecutors together to participate in workshops and lectures to further their knowledge while providing them with the tools necessary to combat the online exploitation of children. Past conference evaluations support our belief that this event provides an unrivaled opportunity to further the education of participants while enhancing their skills to protect America's children.

- 2006 Annual ICAC Silicon Valley Conference (May 31 - June 2, 2006)

  The third annual Silicon Valley ICAC Conference will be held in San Jose, CA May 31 - June 2, 2006. The conference will again offer training in the area of Internet crimes against children, both in lecture and hands-on computer lab instruction. Please register for this conference through the Silicon Valley ICAC.

Other Training

The ICAC Task Force Training and Technical Assistance Program is pleased to list training here that is being offered by Task Force agencies or other ICAC related programs.

- Other ICAC-related Training

Training Partners

Fox Valley Technical College (FVTC) Training Programs
FVTC is funded by a cooperative agreement through the Office of Juvenile Justice and Delinquency Prevention. They provide training to law enforcement, prosecution and social service professionals.

National Center for Missing & Exploited Children (NCMEC) Training Programs
NCMEC was established in 1984 as a private, nonprofit organization to provide services nationwide for families and professionals in the prevention of abducted, endangered, and sexually exploited children. They offer training programs to law enforcement and social service professionals.

SEARCH
SEARCH, the National Consortium for Justice Information and Statistics, helps state and local justice agencies with their information and identification technology needs through effective planning and implementation assistance, high tech crimes investigation training, and criminal history policy.

American Prosecutors Research Institute (APRI)
In 1985, the National District Attorneys Association established the National Center for Prosecution of Child Abuse as a program of the American Prosecutors Research Institute (APRI). Aimed at responding to an increasing volume of reported child abuse, the National Center serves as a central resource for training, expert legal assistance, court reform and state-of-the-art information on criminal child abuse investigations and prosecutions.

[back to top]

Home | About Us | Resources | Training | Contact Us | Site Map

Internet Crimes Against Children Task Force Training & Technical Assistance Program
Page Last Updated: 11/21/2006

III. i-SAFE Internet Safety Education

i-SAFE is a full curriculum of internet safety programs for children, parents and teachers. The curriculum covers kindergarten to 12th grades. The best part about the i-SAFE program is it is funded by a federal grant from OJJDP and they make the training available at no cost to schools and students. That is right, no cost. Every time I do an internet safety presentation at a school, parents and teachers all want to know if they can get more training for their students. I have no problem recommending them to the folks at i-SAFE. To get all the details on this wonderful program visit http://isafe.org.

Take a look at the different types of assistance the site has to offer. Starting with *Kids & Teens* you will see the program does not just use adults to teach internet safety to children. The program has a mentoring program that allows older students to become involved in delivering internet safety training to younger students.

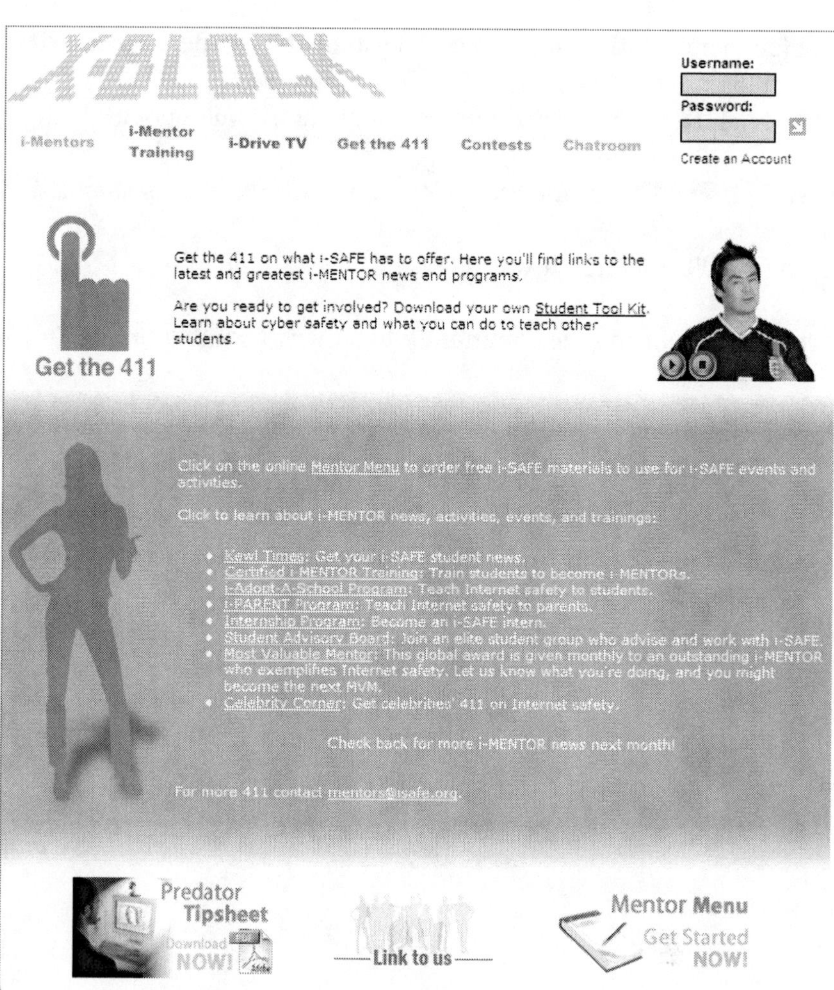

I was fortunate enough to be involved in a day-long internet safety program sponsored by i-SAFE and Microsoft on the campus of the University of California at San Diego. I saw hundreds of students working together to create internet safety messages. They created posters and public service announcements that were recorded in the television studio on campus. The students also performed skits about online predators and internet safety and came up with their own Top Ten List of internet safety tips. This event was attended by over 900 students. It was an excellent example of how i-SAFE brings students and the community together to combat online predators.

On this page you will find a free Predator Tip Sheet.

Predator Tip Sheet

Eluding Internet Predators

One in five children who use computer chat rooms has been approached over the Internet by a pedophile.

Only one in four youth who received a sexual solicitation reported the incident to an adult.

i-SAFE Inc. has created this list of tips and reminders that can be used to help recognize these potentially hazardous situations and to respond appropriately.

- **Keep user names and profiles generic and anonymous.**
  Discuss your child's online screen name, profile, and activities. Many provide too much personal information. Ensure all screen names and profiles are nonspecific.
- **Avoid posting personal photos online.**
  Pictures can be altered to embarrass or humiliate. They also provide personal information that can help an Internet predator act familiar by pretending to know you, your children, and/or their friends.
- **Always keep private information private.**
  With just three pieces of personal information, specialized Internet search engines can be used to locate someone anywhere. Internet conversations should never include any personal information.
- **Place the family computer in an open area.**
  A responsible adult should always accompany minors while they access the Internet to provide support and direction should they be confronted with an aggressive solicitation or inappropriate materials.
- **Remind children that online "friends" are still strangers.**
  Predators trick their victims into believing that they have similar interests and groom children to desire a more intimate relationship. The reality is that online friends are still strangers, and your child can never be sure that the person is who he or she says.
- **Respect children's privacy.**
  Respect your child's privacy, but make certain he or she knows everyone on his or her e-mail or instant messenger "Buddy" list. Work to generate parent and child trust that supports open and honest Internet use.
- **Become a part of your child's online experience.**
  It can be a fun journey to explore the wonders of the Internet as a family. As computer-savvy as kids and teens are today, they will certainly teach you a thing or two!
- **Be aware of phone calls or mail deliveries from unfamiliar persons.**
  Predators often call or send gifts to their potential victims in their process of grooming.
- **Learn about the Internet.**
  The more you know about how the Internet works, the better prepared you are to teach your children about how online predators operate and what you can do together to identify and elude them.
- **Get involved with i-SAFE Inc.**
  Raise Internet safety awareness by joining, creating, or supporting an i-PARENT Board in your school or community, and informing other parents what they can do to keep their families safe online.

1

The Tip Sheet may be a second document you want to pin up in a prominent location by your computer.

The i-SAFE program does not stop there. It has components for *Educators*.

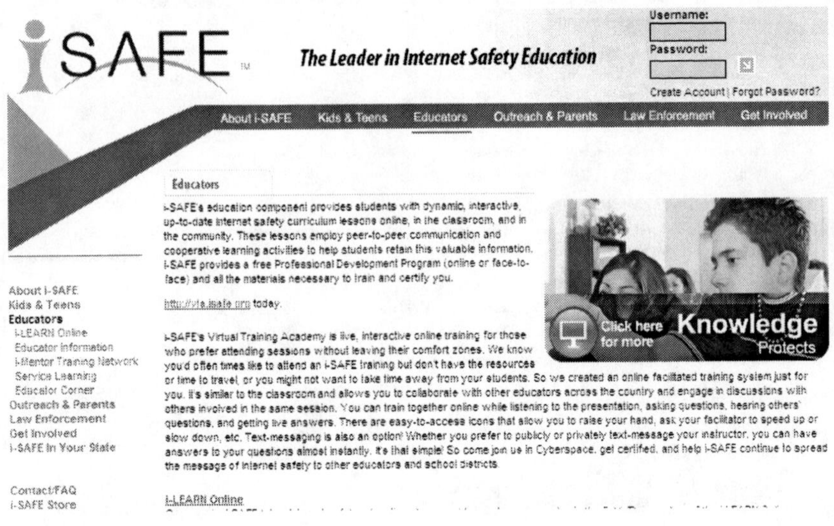

i-SAFE personnel will come to your community and train the educators in your schools to teach the i-SAFE curriculum.

The *Community Outreach & Parents* section is where the mentoring program can be found. This program brings the community into the fight against online predators and explains how older students can help keep younger students safer online.

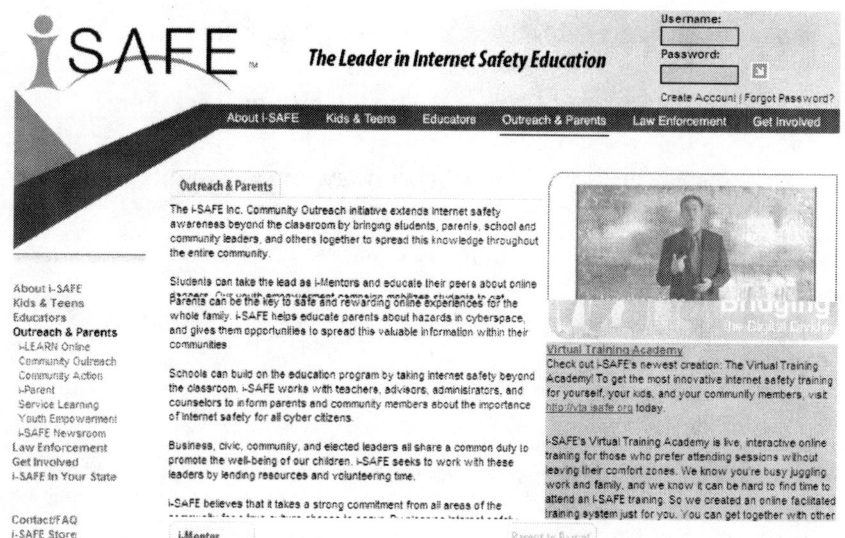

The program also integrates local law enforcement. With this program the folks from i-SAFE train local law enforcement to teach the online predator segment. This way the children hear about these online predators from someone who can answer additional questions about the legality of other activities online. I guarantee the children will be asking about downloading music and movies.

IV. The National Center for Missing and Exploited Children

Thanks to the National Center for Missing and Exploited Children (NCMEC), the Internet Crimes Against Children Task Force (ICAC) has the ability to connect with law enforcement around the world. That connection can ultimately save children from a devastating victimization.

One example was a case where a woman announced in a chat room that she was running a day care center and she was going to molest one of the children in her care. She let everyone in the chat room know she was going to display that molestation via web camera to anyone who wanted to watch. Fortunately, a police officer in Ohio was in that chat room and began investigating the women immediately. The police officer discovered the woman was located somewhere in Illinois. This officer contacted the NCMEC and after some research, they were able to determine her location. They contacted the Illinois Attorney General's Office and with the assistance of the police department in the town where the woman lived, she was stopped and arrested. Subsequently, she was found guilty and sentenced to prison.

Due to the immediate nature of the molestation you can see how valuable NCMEC can be in preventing the victimization of children and as a resource to law enforcement.

But NCMEC is not just there to assist law enforcement. They have many programs to assist children, parents and teachers. NCMEC's website can be found at http://www.ncmec.org/.

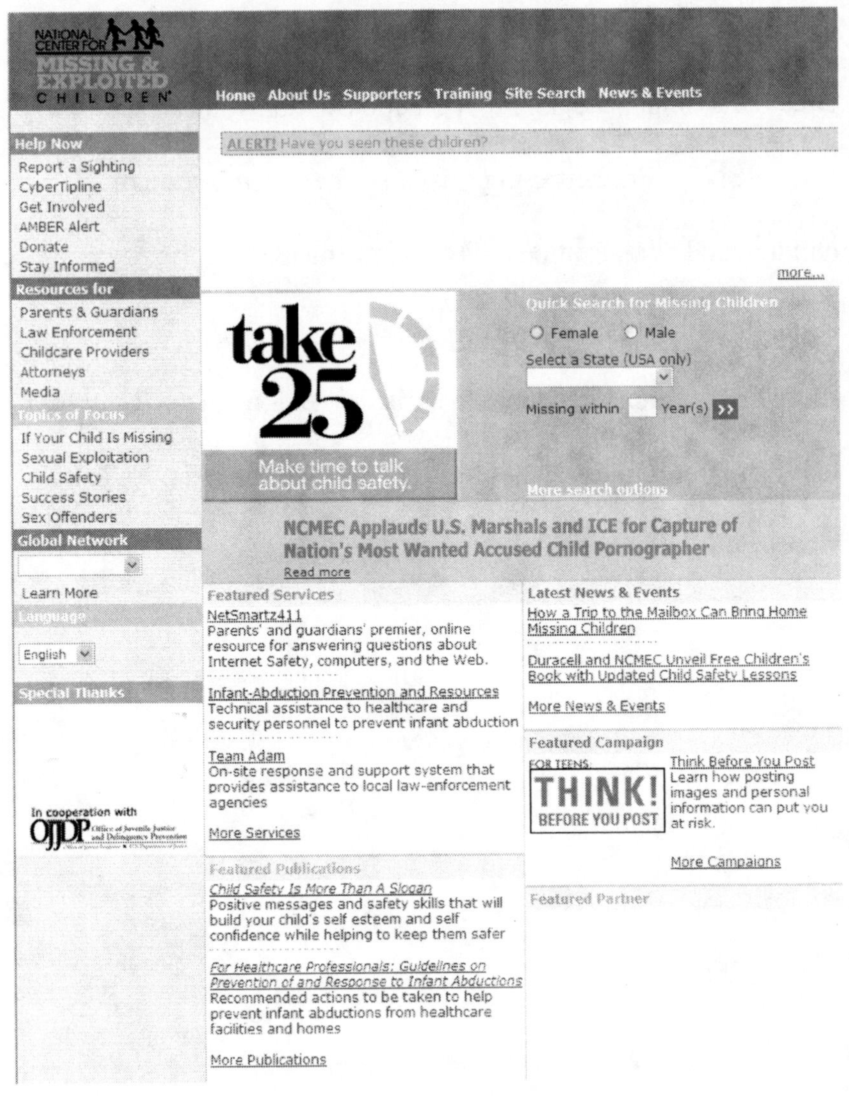

On the upper left section of the page you can see the link to the *CyberTipline*. Anyone can report a suspicious online contact or an online predator through this tipline. If you wish, you can make the report anonymously.

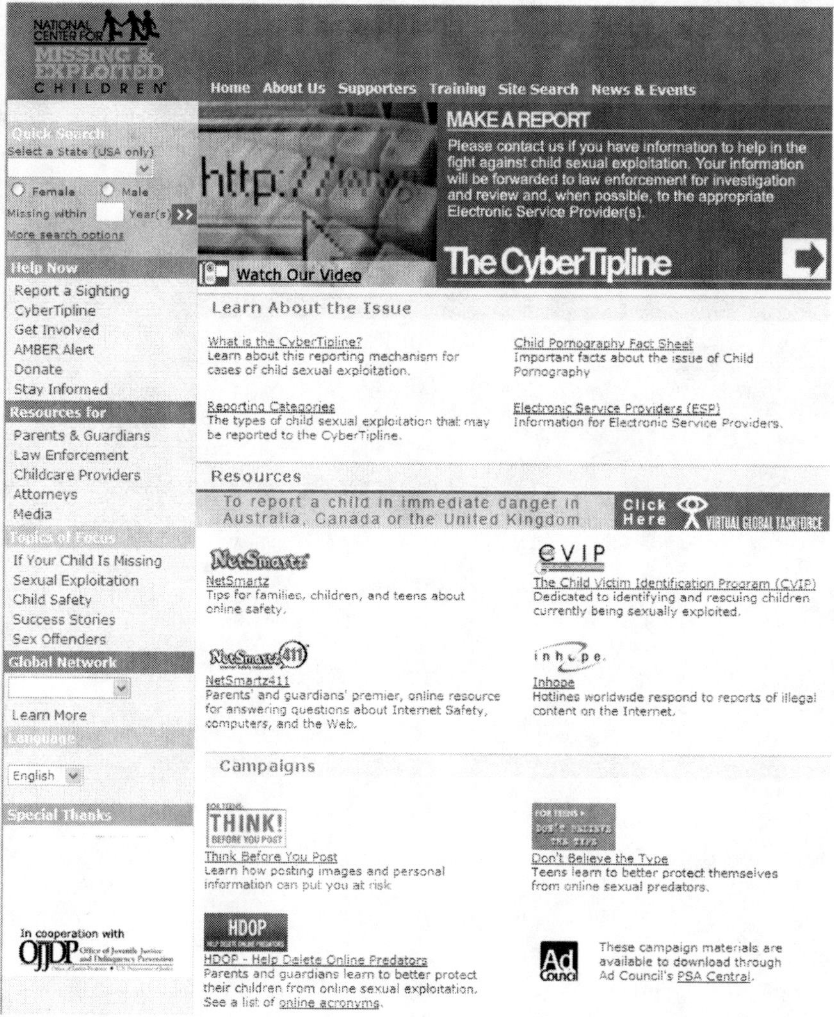

The folks at NCMEC will follow up on the tip and try to find out as much as they can about the online predator before forwarding the tip to law enforcement. They will send the tip, complete with their research data, to a law enforcement agency in the geographical area where the online predator lives.

NATIONAL CENTER FOR MISSING & EXPLOITED CHILDREN

Home About Us Supporters Training Site Search News & Events

Quick Search
Select a State (USA only)
Female Male
Missing within Year(s)
More search options

Help Now
Report a Sighting
CyberTipline
Get Involved
AMBER Alert
Donate
Stay Informed

Resources for
Parents & Guardians
Law Enforcement
Childcare Providers
Attorneys
Media

Topics of Focus
If Your Child Is Missing
Sexual Exploitation
Child Safety
Success Stories
Sex Offenders

Global Network
Learn More

Language
English

Special Thanks

In cooperation with OJJDP Office of Juvenile Justice and Delinquency Prevention

Information entered into this form will be forwarded to law enforcement for investigation and review.
To Submit Information on Missing Children Call 1-800-THE-LOST.

Reporting Person (Help)

Approximate Date and Time of Incident - REQUIRED
Month MM | Day DD | Year YYYY | Hour | Min | Time Zone
01 | 01 | 1900 | 01 | 01 | AM | Alaska

Type of Incident - REQUIRED

Location of Incident (City & State where incident occurred)

First Name | Last Name

Address | City

State *If USA | Postal Code | Country

State *If Not USA | E-mail Address

Phone # (xxx-xxx-xxxx) | Additional Phone # | Time Available for Callback

Relationship to Child

If applicable, please fill in the information below:

Internet Information (Help)

Date and Time Accessed
Month MM | Day DD | Year YYYY | Hour | Min

Reporting spam?

Internet Location (e.g. Newsgroups, FTP, etc.)

Website/HTTP/URL/FTP
http://

Chatroom: Name or Location if not IRC

IRC Channel Name | IRC Server Name

FServe Trigger

HTTP/FTP Login | HTTP/FTP Password

E-mail/Newsgroup Header

Logs of Conversation?

If applicable, please fill in the information below:

Child Victim (Help)

First Name | Last Name

Address | City

State *If USA | Postal Code | Country

State *If Not USA | E-mail Address

Date of Birth (mm/dd/yyyy) | Approximate Age * | Other Children?

If applicable, please fill in the following information:

Suspect (Help)

First Name | Last Name

Address | City

State *If USA | Postal Code | Country

State *If Not USA | Approximate Age

E-mail Address

Screen/User Name | ICQ # | IP Address

* Other Suspects?

Law Enforcement Information (Help)

Incident Has Been Reported to Law Enforcement

Agency Name

Officer's First Name | Officer's Last Name

Officer's Phone # (xxx-xxx-xxxx)

Additional Information (Help)

Please provide additional information or description (be specific). If reporting multiple websites, please limit to 5 in each report.
*Other victims or suspects should be listed in this section

Submit

Also available from the NCMEC home page is the AMBER Alert. Click on the *AMBER Alert* link and it will take you to the web page explaining how the AMBER Alert functions.

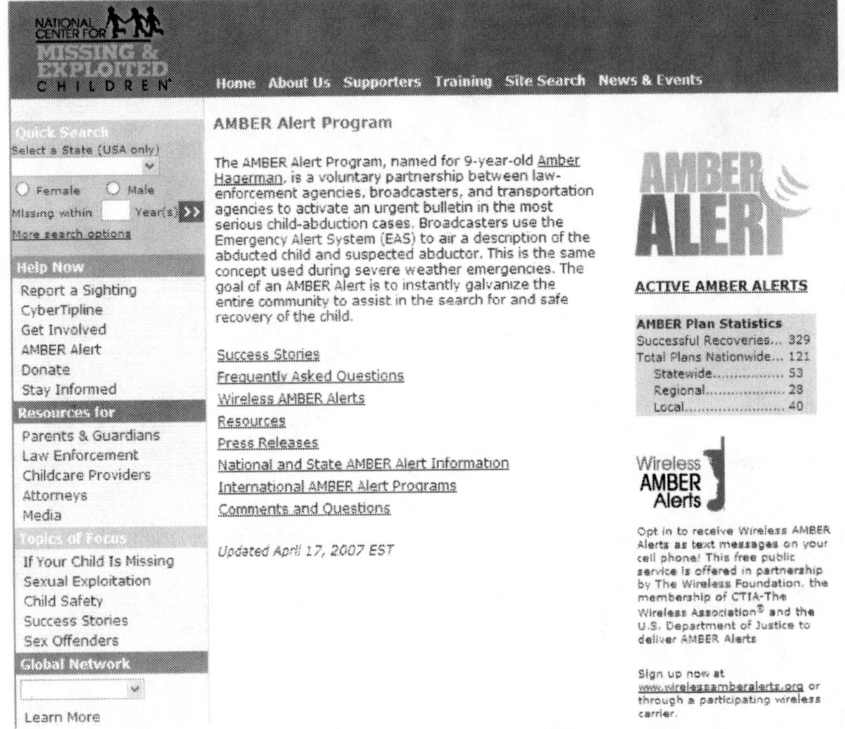

Click on the large *AMBER Alert* on the upper right side of the page and you will see the information on any current AMBER Alerts.

As you can see, at the time I checked the site there were no active AMBER Alerts. That is a good thing.

Look through the *Teens* section for the videos and true stories and take some time to check out the *Resources for Parents & Guardians*. Try looking at the advice on babysitters or day care. There is so much help on this page, it is impossible to recount all of it here.

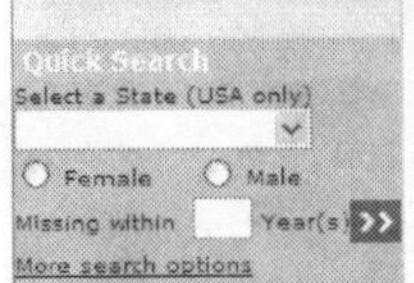

Home About Us Supporters Training Site Search News & Events

Quick Search
Select a State (USA only)
Female Male
Missing within Year(s)
More search options

Help Now
Report a Sighting
CyberTipline
Get Involved
AMBER Alert
Donate
Stay Informed

Resources for
Parents & Guardians
Law Enforcement
Childcare Providers
Attorneys
Media

Topics of Focus
If Your Child Is Missing
Sexual Exploitation
Child Safety
Success Stories
Sex Offenders

Global Network
Learn More

Language
English

Special Thanks

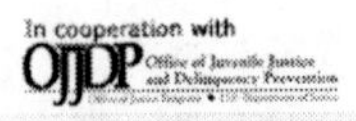

Resources for Parents & Guardians

We want to help you protect your children by teaching them to be smarter and safer. The best way to combat child exploitation and abduction is to prevent it. Please use our site to learn what you and your children need to know about protecting them from victimization.

- What to do If Your Child Is Missing
- Information about International Abduction
- Where to Report Child Sexual Exploitation
- Child-Sexual-Exploitation State Resources
- Learn About Keeping Your Child Safer
- Learn about how to stay safer online with the NetSmartz Workshop
- Learn about the importance of having a good quality photo of your child
- Corporate Partner Safety Programs and Materials
- Learn about "Prevention Works," a Work-Life Benefit for Employees/Employers

Parents' and guardians' premier, online resource for answering questions about Internet Safety, computers, and the Web. Visit NetSmartz411.org.

Featured Services

24-Hour Hotline
Code Adam
Family-Reunification Services
Infant-Abduction Prevention and Resources
NetSmartz

More Services

Featured Publications

A Family Resource Guide on International Parental Kidnapping
Blog Beware
Family Abduction
Is this your CHILD? If not--it may be NEXT TIME
Just in Case...Babysitter
Just in Case...Daycare
Just in Case...Runaway
Know the Rules...Abduction and Kidnapping Prevention Tips for Parents and Guardians
Know the Rules...After-School Safety Tips for Children Who Are Home Alone
Know the Rules...General Tips for Parents and Guardians to Help Keep Their Children Safer
Parental Guidelines in Case Your Child Might Someday be the Victim of Sexual Exploitation.
Personal Safety for Children: A Guide for Parents
Preventing the Sexual Exploitation of Children
When Your Child is Missing: A Family Survival Guide

More Publications

Many of the topics have pamphlets that you can print out free of charge. Also NCMEC will also supply up to 50 copies of the pamphlets at no cost. This comes in handy when you're trying to supply enough pamphlets to each member of your child's fifth grade class.

Try looking through the *Frequently Asked Questions* (FAQs) to assist you in talking to your child about online dangers. Most likely, you will find the answer to many of your children's questions within these FAQs.

NetSmartz Workshop

Keeping Kids and Teens Safer on the Internet

Parents/Guardians Educators LawEnforcement Teens Kids Español

Learn About the Issue
- Online Risks
- Definitions
- Internet Safety News
- Statistics
- Public-Service Announcements

Keep Kids & Teens Safer
- Ask Dr. Sharon
- Use Your NetSmartz
- Safety Pledges
- Safety Tips
- Real-Life Stories

Teach Internet Safety
- Activity Cards
- On/Offline Activities
- Recommended Resources

Watch Videos
- Real-Life Stories
- Ask Dr. Sharon
- Public-Service Announcements

About NetSmartz
- About Us
- How to Use NetSmartz
- Accolades
- Sponsors
- Press Releases
- Contact Us
- Link to Us

Parents & Guardians

Communication is an effective tool for parents and guardians when helping their children avoid the dangers that exist on the Internet. NetSmartz provides on- and offline learning activities for parents to facilitate discussions with their children and teens about Internet safety. Visit "Parent FAQ" to learn more about how and why parents should use NetSmartz.

Features

NetSmartz411

NetSmartz411 is a parent and guardian's premier, online resource for learning about Internet safety, computers, and the Web.

Search our knowledge base for answers to all of your questions about the online world! If you can't find what you're looking for, use the "Ask the Experts" tab to send us a question.

Your question will be answered by professionals who know a lot about Internet safety – the real-life analysts at the National Center for Missing & Exploited Children. We handle daily reports about the online exploitation of children; and we'll show you the steps you can take to keep the children and teens in your life safer online.

Visit NetSmartz411.org.

Real-World Safety

Teach your children how to be safer both on- and offline. Videos to address real-world safety for children are now available at NetSmartzKids.org.

Visit NetSmartzKids.org.

Dr. Sharon

Developmental pediatrician Dr. Sharon Cooper teaches parents and guardians how to help protect children from victimization.

Watch Dr. Sharon videos.

CyberTipline Report

Has your child ever been sent inappropriate material by someone he or she met online? Has your child ever inadvertently encountered inappropriate material? These are all types of child sexual exploitation. Make a report at CyberTipline.com or by calling 1.800.THE.LOST if you have information that will help in our fight against child sexual exploitation.

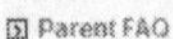

CyberTipline

Parent FAQ

Do you know who to contact if your child is asked to meet in person? Get suggestions for what to do if your child encounters a possibly dangerous situation online.

Parent FAQ

Links

Blog Beware

NetSmartz Kids

Activity Cards

Commonly Used Lingo

Free Stuff

Besides looking through the FAQs you can also “Ask the Experts” and the folks at NCMEC will get you an answer. This program is similar to the i-SAFE program to help **educators** and **law enforcement**.

NCMEC also has a full curriculum available for students, parents, teachers and law enforcement. Through their NetSmartz program you can receive training to teach these classes in your community.

Younger children will also benefit from using NCMEC’s interactive NetSmartz program. The program uses cartoon characters to teach children about the dangers on the internet. You will meet people with names like Clicky, Nettie and Webster. They will help to teach your children about the dangers online. Through this program, children learn about how to deal with bad guys like Potty Mouth Pete. The interactive cartoons give children the skills to deal with people who use foul language, ask personal questions or say mean things online.

NetSmartzKids™
Home
Games
Activities
E-Mail
Use Your NetSmartz
Free Stuff
Tunes
Parents
Teens
Educators
Law Enforcement
Click here!
Send
Choose a category.
NetSmartz
NOW
TUNES
CLICK HERE TO JOIN
CLICKY & ALYSON STONER
Clicky's Pick
E-Cards
INTERNET
Clicky's Stolen Song:
A Lesson in Digital Ethics
Captain Bootleg, an Internet pirate, has stolen Clicky's hit song. Nettie and Webster learn why it is wrong to steal music from others. Play Scavenger Hunt after you watch the show to help Clicky find his stolen CDs.
E-Cards
Help your friends learn to UYN (Use Your NetSmartz). Send an E-card!
Who's Your Friend
on the Internet?
Nettie and Webster explain the dangers of the Internet in this game show.
E-Mail a Character
If you are a Mac user, click here!
Clicky's Quest
The mysterious Baron E. Vyle has freed the Webville Outlaws. Capture all of the Outlaws and advance to the next level!
Scavenger Hunt
Help Nettie and Webster collect all the missing CDs. Find hidden treasures and meet new characters for clues to help you.
Maze Game
Navigate Clicky through the maze and eat the computer chips while avoiding the Webville Outlaws. Along the way find trusted adults for power boosts.
About Us
Contact Us
Privacy Policy

Take some time to play a few of the games with your child. The games are not only fun, but they are also very educational, even for parents. I have to admit that I learned some very valuable information from playing the games and hearing the questions children ask about what occurred in the game. They make a great format for teaching internet safety to a third or fourth grade class.

At times, I have referred to several reports that were sponsored by the Department of Justice, the Office of Juvenile Justice and Delinquency Prevention and the Crimes Against Children Research Center at the University of New Hampshire. Click on *Site Search* and type in "online victimization" or "five years later." Links to those reports will be displayed. You can read the reports online or click on the link to download and print out the report.

Home About Us Supporters Training Site Search News & Events

online victimization GO

Quick Search
Select a State (USA only)
Female Male
Missing within Year(s)
More search options

Help Now
Report a Sighting
CyberTipline
Get Involved
AMBER Alert
Donate
Stay Informed

Resources for
Parents & Guardians
Law Enforcement
Childcare Providers
Attorneys
Media

Topics of Focus
If Your Child Is Missing
Sexual Exploitation
Child Safety
Success Stories
Sex Offenders

Global Network
Learn More

Language
English

Special Thanks

In cooperation with OJJDP Office of Juvenile Justice and Delinquency Prevention

Matched **94** pages in **0.06** seconds

1. *Online Victimization*: A Report on the Nation's Youth (2000)
   Home About Us Supporters Training Site Search News & Events Quick Search Select a State (USA only) Alabama Alaska Arizona Arkansas California Colorado Connecticut Delaware District of Columbia Florida Georgia Guam Hawaii Idaho Illinois
   ... **Online Victimization**: A Report on the Nation's Youth (2000) ...
   - 20k cache

2. *Online Victimization* of Youth: Five Years Later (2006)
   Home About Us Supporters Training Site Search News & Events Quick Search Select a State (USA only) Alabama Alaska Arizona Arkansas California Colorado Connecticut Delaware District of Columbia Florida Georgia Guam Hawaii Idaho Illinois
   ... **Online Victimization** of Youth: Five Years Later (2006) ...
   - 20k cache

3. Collier County Announces a Collaborative Effort to Help Protect Children from *Online Victimization*
   Home About Us Supporters Training Site Search News & Events Quick Search Select a State (USA only) Alabama Alaska Arizona Arkansas California Colorado Connecticut Delaware District of Columbia Florida Georgia Guam Hawaii Idaho Illinois
   ... Children from **Online Victimization** ...
   - 24k cache

4. New Study Shows Youth *Online* Exposed to More Sexual Material and Harassment
   Home About Us Supporters Training Site Search News & Events Quick Search Select a State (USA only) Alabama Alaska Arizona Arkansas California Colorado Connecticut Delaware District of Columbia Florida Georgia Guam Hawaii Idaho Illinois
   ... of Solicitation **Online Victimization** of Youth: Five Years Later Alexandria, VA & Durham, NH – ...
   - 24k cache

5. Qwest and NCMEC Join Colorado Leaders to Help Fight Internet Crimes Against Children
   Home About Us Supporters Training Site Search News & Events Quick Search Select a State (USA only) Alabama Alaska Arizona Arkansas California Colorado Connecticut Delaware District of Columbia Florida Georgia Guam Hawaii Idaho Illinois
   ... the incidence of **online victimization**. Qwest has created a coalition of key leaders, who are united ...
   - 28k cache

6. Department of Justice Announces Partnership with Ad Council and NCMEC in PSA Campaign
   Home About Us Supporters Training Site Search News & Events Quick Search Select a State (USA only) Alabama Alaska Arizona Arkansas California Colorado Connecticut Delaware District of Columbia Florida Georgia Guam Hawaii Idaho Illinois
   ... them at risk for **online victimization**. The sexual **victimization** of children - including child porno ...
   - 25k cache

7. DC's Attorney General Offers Kids the Tools They Need to Stay Safer *Online*
   Home About Us Supporters Training Site Search News & Events Quick Search Select a State (USA only) Alabama Alaska Arizona Arkansas California Colorado Connecticut Delaware District of Columbia Florida Georgia Guam Hawaii Idaho Illinois
   ... to NCMEC's **Online Victimization**: A Report on the Nation's Youth, approximately 1 in 5 c ...
   - 20k cache

8. Qwest and NCMEC Join Washington Leaders to Help Fight Internet Crimes Against Children
   Home About Us Supporters Training Site Search News & Events Quick Search Select a State (USA only) Alabama Alaska Arizona Arkansas California Colorado Connecticut Delaware District of Columbia Florida Georgia Guam Hawaii Idaho Illinois
   ... the incidence of **online victimization**. "The Washington Attorney General's office has wo ...
   - 26k cache

9. *Online* Enticement - What it is
   Home About Us Supporters Training Site Search News & Events Quick Search Select a State (USA only) Alabama Alaska Arizona Arkansas California Colorado Connecticut Delaware District of Columbia Florida Georgia Guam Hawaii Idaho Illinois
   ... David Finkelhor. **Online Victimization** of Youth: Five Years Later. Alexandria, Virginia. National Ce ...

CONCLUSION

My intention in writing this book was to give parents an understanding of the dangers that may exist in the online communities their children frequent. I know that some of the content of this book may be shocking to some parents, and by now you are probably thinking about throwing your computer out the window. This would be a huge mistake and it will hurt your children in the long run. Please do not become frustrated. Your children need to use the computer and the internet to gain skills so that they can compete in school and ultimately in the workplace.

Take solace in knowing that millions of children access the internet, social networking sites and instant messaging sessions every day with no negative contact. Remember the statistics: one in seven children reported unwanted sexual contact. That means for every bad experience online, six children had a pleasant one. Instead of fearing the computer and the internet, realize that with a little vigilance on your part and an open line of communication, your children can enjoy a safe and happy online experience.

Talk to your children frequently about their online habits. Realize that as they grow older, their use of the computer and the internet will change. Be willing to change their authorization to see or visit sites on the internet or use instant messaging as they demonstrate the maturity to handle new freedoms. Try not to take away the computer or internet as a form of punishment. If your children associate punishment with loss of computer and internet privileges, they may become secretive about where they visit online and what social networking profiles they have created. If they start to believe keeping secrets from you is a good thing, they are playing right into the online predator's hands.

My goal was to make parents aware of how online predators use computers, chat rooms, instant messaging, social networking sites and online dating sites to locate and groom their victims. Knowledge is power, and when it comes to your children and online predators, knowledge is not only power, it is an absolute necessity for parents. Knowing how to check your computer for chat, instant messaging programs and online profiles is imperative. If you find these types of programs, have a discussion with your child. Ask them to explain how they use the programs and with whom they may be communicating. Check the types of pictures on their profiles and explain why some may not be appropriate or could cause them difficulties later in life. Check for personal information and explain how this could cause them to be contacted in person or to become the victim of identity theft.

If you believe your child has been the victim of an online predator report it immediately. I have given you several ways to report online crimes. The easiest way is to contact the National Center for Missing and Exploited Children (NCMEC), fill out a CyberTip and allow NCMEC to get the information into the hands of a computer-literate police officer. Do not feel hesitant to report such online conduct. I know from my own experience and from speaking with many other police officers, we would rather follow up on many tips that do not end in an arrest than miss one tip and have a child harmed.

Remember the strongest weapon an online predator has against your child is secrecy. The strongest weapon a parent has against online predators is communication. Take the time to talk to your children.

CHAT GLOSSARY

The following is an abbreviated list of chat terms. For a more in-depth list of chat terms I recommend you launch your browser, type in www.google.com, then in the search box type chat abbreviations. There will be a host of sites with hundreds of examples. New abbreviations are constantly being created. The best way to know what is meant when an abbreviation is used by your child is to ask your child.

143 I love you
411 information
420 marijuana
911 parent in room-stop talking-not safe someone is watching
AFK away from keyboard
A/S/L age/sex/location
A/S/L/P age/sex/location/do you have a picture of you to send
BAK back at keyboard
BF boyfriend
BFF best friends forever
BFN bye for now
BRB be right back
BTW by the way
CUL8R see you later
FAQ frequently asked questions
GF girlfriend
IDK I don't know
IDKY I don't know you
ILU I love you
IM instant message
IRL in real life
JC just checking
JK just kidding
JO jerk off/masturbation
KEWL cool

L8R	later
LMIRL	let's meet in real life
LOL	laugh out loud
M/F	male or female
MIRL	meet in real life
NP	no problem
NW	no way
OIC	oh I see
P2P	peer to peer
P911	parents are present
PM	private message
RL	real life-as in meet me in real life
ROFL	rolling on floor laughing
RP	role playing
RU	are you
SN	screen name
STR8	straight
SUP	what is up
THX	thanks
TM	trust me
TTYL	talk to you later
TY	thank you
YW	you are welcome

Another form of chat abbreviations is referred to as emoticons. Key strokes are combined to convey an emotion. If you turn your head to the left you can decipher some of the emoticons. In some chat clients the key strokes are displayed as pictures of the emotion conveyed. Below are just a few examples.

:-)	smiling
:-D	laughing
:*	kiss or kissing
;-)	winking
:-O	surprised
>:)	devilish grin or evil grin
:-(	sad

:-x	in love
>:-<	angry
:-P	tongue sticking out
>:D<	hug
[]	hug

To obtain a more in-depth listing of these emoticons try searching the term emoticon on Google.